D1737477

**JANE'S POCKET BOOK OF
HOME-BUILT AIRCRAFT**

JANE'S POCKET BOOK OF
HOME-BUILT AIRCRAFT

Compiled by Michael J. H. Taylor
Edited by John W. R. Taylor FRHist S, AFRAe S, FSLAET

COLLIER BOOKS
A Division of Macmillan Publishing Co., Inc.
New York

Macmillan Publishing Co., Inc.
866 Third Avenue, New York, N.Y. 10022
Collier Macmillan Canada, Ltd.

Library of Congress Cataloging in Publication Data
Main entry under title:
Jane's Pocket book of home-built aircraft.
(Jane's pocket books)
1. Airplanes, Home-built—Catalogs. I. Taylor,
Michael John Haddrick. II. Taylor, John William Ransom.
III. Title: Pocket book of home-built aircraft.
TL514.J36   629.133   77-5412
ISBN 0-02-080650-7

First Collier Books Edition 1977

Printed in the United States of America

FOREWORD

TL5/4
.J36

With the spirit of adventure that inspired early pioneers of aviation, more and more people throughout the world are using their skills, time and money to produce aircraft that revive the magic of "real flying" in an age of fast but tedious air travel in expensive high-flying airliners. Not content to buy a factory-constructed type, as described in the companion *Jane's Pocket Book of Light Aircraft,* these modern pioneers are completely happy only when they can soar through the sky in a machine which they have built with their own hands and, in many cases, designed themselves.

It would be a mistake to consider such homebuilts as foolhardy runabouts, and their designers as daredevils. Each is designed and built to high standards, with the care and integrity required of a major manufacturer. All have to pass strict inspection before they are awarded a Permit to Fly, and some homebuilts are fully aerobatic. Their capability is underlined by the fact that the Pitts Special, victor in World Aerobatic Contests, is among the types described and illustrated in this book.

So, what exactly is a "homebuilt"? Generally speaking, it is an aircraft that is not assembled on a production line or sold in completed form but is built, with the aid of plans, from parts or raw materials. Many are "one-offs" built for the personal enjoyment of their designer-builders; others are produced by large numbers of individual amateur constructors, through the sale of plans, components and materials. A few are of such quality that they become production types, manufactured professionally by major companies.

The significance of homebuilts is emphasised by the fact that a large self-contained section of *Jane's All the World's Aircraft* is now devoted to such types. This is well justified, and no other branch of aviation offers such a rich variety of shapes and sizes, including the futuristic Rutan VariEze and VariViggen, the Hovey Whing Ding and PDQ-2 which are little more than flying seats, and the highly sophisticated Bede BD-5J single-seat homebuilt jet. Also to be found in this Pocket Book are scaled-down flying replicas of First and Second World War fighters like the de Havilland D.H.2, Focke-Wulf Fw 190, Supermarine Spitfire and Hawker Hurricane, which keep alive for their constructor-pilots memories of the most dramatic periods of flying history.

Often the homebuilts themselves have fascinating backgrounds. For example, the first of some 200 Pazmany PL-4As destined for use by Canadian Air Cadets are being built by inmates of a local civil prison. These men will also produce components for the remaining PL-4As, which will then be assembled by the Cadets themselves.

By providing details of virtually all designs available to amateur constructors, and some of the more interesting new "one-offs", this Pocket Book forms a unique and valuable companion for earlier books in the series, devoted to products of the professional aerospace industry. It should never be forgotten that the first aircraft built by the founders of that industry – men like the Wright brothers, Curtiss, de Havilland, Handley Page, A.V. Roe, Blériot and Sikorsky – were all homebuilts.

MICHAEL J.H. TAYLOR

Single-seat ultra-light monoplane

Power plant: One 26 kW (35 hp) 785 cc Toyota 2U-1 motor car engine
Wing span: 7.50 m (24 ft 7¼ in)
Wing area, gross: 9.00 m² (96.9 sq ft)
Length overall: 5.50 m (18 ft 0½ in)
Height over tail: 2.20 m (7 ft 2¾ in)
Weight empty: 180 kg (397 lb)
Max T-O weight: 265 kg (584 lb)
Max level speed: 42.5 knots (79 km/h; 49 mph)
Max rate of climb at S/L: 72 m (236 ft)/min

Service ceiling: 1,500 m (4,920 ft)
Max range: 37.8 nm (70 km; 43.5 miles)
Accommodation: Exposed seat with harness
Construction: Wooden wing and tail unit, fabric covered. 'Cockpit' and wing support structure of aluminium alloy. Rear fuselage of wooden construction, plywood covered. Non-retractable landing gear

History: The Mizet II single-seat homebuilt aircraft was built between 1968 and 1973 by a team of students at Kushiro Technical High School, Hokkaido, led by Mr Keiichi Abe, its designer. It made its first flight in December 1973. A Mizet III is under construction

Single-seat light monoplane

Data: Version with 48.5 kW (65 hp) engine
Power plant: One Continental A65, A85, C65 or C85 flat-four engine of 48.5-63.5 kW (65-85 hp)
Wing span: 8.05 m (26 ft 5 in)
Wing area, gross: 10.43 m² (112.3 sq ft)
Length overall: 5.40 m (17 ft 8¾ in)
Height overall: 2.02 m (6 ft 7¾ in)
Weight empty, equipped: 261 kg (575 lb)
Max T-O weight: 431 kg (950 lb)
Max level speed at S/L: 96 knots (177 km/h; 110 mph)
Max cruising speed: 87-91 knots (160-169 km/h; 100-105 mph)
Max rate of climb at S/L: 365 m (1,200 ft)/min
Service ceiling: 4,875 m (16,000 ft)
Range with max fuel: 303 nm (560 km; 350 miles)
Accommodation: Single seat in open cockpit. Space for 4.5 kg (10 lb) of baggage
Construction: Braced wooden wing, fabric covered. Welded steel tube fuselage and tail unit, fabric covered. Non-retractable landing gear

History: The Baby Ace was manufactured originally in 1931, in kit form, by Corben Aircraft Company, which had been established in 1923. The Corben assets were acquired in 1953 by Mr Paul Poberezny who, with the help of Mr S.J. Dzik, completely redesigned the Baby Ace, with the intention of offering it in the form of plans and kits of parts for amateur construction. All rights in the new version, known as the Model C, were sold to Mr Cliff DuCharme. Again the Baby Ace was redesigned, as the Model D, and special tools were built to produce Baby Ace components in quantity. At the same time the two-seat Junior Ace was redesigned as the Junior Ace Model E. In 1961 the company was acquired by Mr Edwin T. Jacob, from whom all rights were purchased by the present owner, Mr Thurman G. Baird, in 1965.

The prototype of the redesigned Baby Ace Model D flew for the first time on 15 November 1956. Large numbers have since been built by amateurs, some of whom have introduced authorised refinements to the basic design. At least one Baby Ace is flying with float landing gear

For details: 106 Arthur Road, Asheville, North Carolina 28806, USA.

Model D with 48.5 kW (65 hp) Continental engine

Single-seat light sporting monoplane

Power plant: Suitable for installation of engines from 44.5-74.5 kW (60-100 hp). Prototype has 51 kW (68 hp) Limbach 1,900 cc flat-four engine
Wing span, standard: 5.94 m (19 ft 6 in)
Wing span, with optional extended wing panels: 7.77 m (25 ft 6 in)
Length overall: 4.88 m (16 ft 0 in)
Height over fuselage: 1.24 m (4 ft 1 in)
Weight empty, extended wing version: 236 kg (520 lb)
Max T-O weight: 340 kg (750 lb)
Never-exceed speed, estimated: 260 knots (482 km/h; 300 mph)
Max cruising speed, estimated: 130 knots (241 km/h; 150 mph)
Max rate of climb at S/L: 366 m (1,200 ft)/min
Range: over 434 nm (804 km; 500 miles)
G limits: ± 9
Accommodation: Single semi-reclined moulded glassfibre bucket seat beneath sideways-opening transparent canopy. Seat folds forward to provide access to baggage space
Construction: All-metal basic structure. Glassfibre fuselage shell.

Electrically-retractable landing gear

History: The Mini-Imp is a single-seat version of the Aerocar Imp. The basic structure is all-metal and is assembled with bolts and pop-rivets, thereby eliminating the need for welding skill.
By early 1976 the Mini-Imp prototype had completed about 40 flying hours. During the Winter of 1975/76 Aerocar built for it a folding wing, which folds in a similar way to that of the Imp. This permits the builder to construct the aircraft in small areas. Aerocar has released drawings of the wing for amateur construction, and several builders hoped to have their Mini-Imps flying by the late Summer of 1976. At the beginning of that year Aerocar was constructing two more pro-totypes, one powered by a 61 kW (82 hp) Kawasaki motorcycle engine and the other by a Continental O-200 engine. The folding wing is at present fitted to the original prototype for test flying.
The extended wing panels to which reference is made in the data, are intended to simplify the owner/builder's task during early solo flights, by permitting lower take-off and landing speeds. When experience has been gained, they can be removed easily and replaced with standard wings

For details: Box 1171, Longview, Washington 98632, USA.

Two-seat light amphibian

Power plant: One 134 kW (180 hp) Franklin 335 engine in prototype. Other power plants installed by amateur constructors include the 164 kW (220 hp) Continental IO-360
Wing span: 10.97 m (36 ft 0 in)
Wing area, gross: 16.72 m² (180 sq ft)
Length overall: 6.10-6.71 m (20 ft 0 in-22 ft 0 in)
Height overall: 2.44 m (8 ft 0 in)
Width folded: 2.44 m (8 ft 0 in)
Weight empty: 499 kg (1,100 lb)
Max T-O weight: 884 kg (1,950 lb)
Never-exceed speed: 120 knots (223 km/h; 139 mph)
Max cruising speed: 113 knots (209 km/h; 130 mph)
Max rate of climb at S/L: 381 m (1,250 ft)/min
Accommodation: Two seats side by side in enclosed cabin
Construction: Structure basically of wood, but tailboom and tail unit can be of steel tube and fabric, wood monocoque or all metal.

Several glassfibre components. Retractable landing gear

History: Known originally as the Coot Model A, the prototype of this aircraft was later renamed Sooper-Coot Model A and flew for the first time in February 1971. It completed approximately 100 flying hours with the originally-installed 89.5 kW (120 hp) Franklin 225 engine before being re-engined with a Franklin 335
The 'float-wing' configuration of the Sooper-Coot permits rough-water operation and, since the close proximity of the wings to the water forms a 'pressure wedge', unusually low take-off and landing speeds are possible without recourse to flaps or other lift-enhancing devices
Certain component parts (including the glassfibre engine cowl, glassfibre hull shell, foredeck, instrument panel, tail fairings, engine cooling-fan blades and steel spring main landing gear legs), and plans, are available to amateur constructors. Over 400 Sooper-Coots are being constructed and 14 were flying by early 1976

For details: Box 1171, Longview, Washington 98632, USA.

(USA)

AEROSPORT QUAIL

Single-seat lightweight cabin monoplane

Power plant: One 1,600 cc modified Volkswagen motor car engine
Wing span: 7.32 m (24 ft 0 in)
Wing area, gross: 7.8 m² (84 sq ft)
Length overall: 4.85 m (15 ft 11 in)
Height overall: 1.69 m (5 ft 6½ in)
Weight empty: 242 kg (534 lb)
Max T-O weight: 359 kg (792 lb)
Max level speed at S/L: 113 knots (209 km/h; 130 mph)
Max cruising speed: 100 knots (185 km/h; 115 mph)
Max rate of climb at S/L: 259 m (850 ft)/min
Service ceiling (estimated): 3,660 m (12,000 ft)
Range with max fuel, no reserve: 200 nm (370 km; 230 miles)
Accommodation: Single seat in enclosed cabin, which is heated.
Space for 9 kg (20 lb) of baggage

Construction: Wing construction as for Aerosport Rail (*which see*). Semi-monocoque all-metal fuselage. All-metal tail unit. Non-retractable landing gear

History: Though very different in appearance to the Rail, the Quail has a similar wing and the same type of landing gear. Its design was started in January 1970, and construction of the prototype began in July 1971. It flew for the first time in December 1971.
The prototype had an all-moving tailplane, but Mr Woods, the designer and builder, evolved a fixed-incidence tailplane with elevators before plans and construction kits were made available to amateur constructors. About 250 sets of plans had been sold by early 1976. Twenty-two Quails were then under construction and six were flying

For details: Box 278, Holly Springs, North Carolina 27540, USA.

Single-seat lightweight monoplane

Power plant: One Volkswagen modified motor car engine of 1,600 to 2,100 cc
Wing span: 7.10 m (23 ft 3½ in)
Wing area, gross: 7.57 m² (81.5 sq ft)
Length overall: 4.80 m (15 ft 9 in)
Height overall: 1.83 m (6 ft 0 in)
Weight empty: 203 kg (446 lb)
Max T-O weight: 331 kg (730 lb)
Max level speed at S/L: 78 knots (145 km/h; 90 mph)
Max cruising speed: 69 knots (129 km/h; 80 mph)
Max rate of climb at S/L: 335 m (1,100 ft)/min
Service ceiling (calculated): 3,660 m (12,000 ft)
Range: 191 nm (354 km; 220 miles)
Accommodation: Single seat in open position
Construction: All-metal construction. Non-retractable landing gear

History: In January 1970 Mr H.L. Woods set out to design an aircraft that would be as simple as possible for construction by amateur builders, requiring no specialised knowledge of constructional techniques or the need for a comprehensive selection of tools. Special emphasis was also placed on safety, ease of handling and maintenance, and economy in operation. The appearance of the aircraft suggested the name Rail.

Construction of the prototype began in May 1970 and the first flight was made on 4 November of that year. FAA certification in the Experimental Category was awarded on 24 June 1971.

The prototype Rail was powered originally by two 24.5 kW (33 hp) modified snowmobile engines. Later, the design was modified to utilise a single Volkswagen modified motor car engine. Plans, a constructional manual and kits of materials and components are available to amateur constructors, and 175 sets of plans had been sold by 1976. At least six Rails were then under construction and two were flying. Aerobatics and spins are prohibited

For details: Box 278, Holly Springs, North Carolina 27540, USA.

Single-seat light biplane

Data: Apply basically to prototype

Power plant: Prototype has one 44.5 kW (60 hp) 1,834 cc Volkswagen modified motor car engine. Design suitable for Volkswagen engine of 1,600 cc to 2,100 cc

Wing span: 5.33 m (17 ft 6 in)

Wing area, gross: 9.52 m² (102.5 sq ft)

Length overall: 4.27 m (14 ft 0 in)

Height overall: 1.69 m (5 ft 6½ in)

Weight empty: 236 kg (520 lb)

Max T-O weight: 348 kg (768 lb)

Max level speed: 82 knots (153 km/h; 95 mph)

Cruising speed: 74 knots (137 km/h; 85 mph)

Service ceiling, (estimated): 3,660 m (12,000 ft)

Range at cruising speed: 130 nm (241 km; 150 miles)

Accommodation: Single seat in open cockpit

Construction: Braced all-metal construction. Non-retractable landing gear

History: The prototype Scamp flew for the first time on 21 August 1973. It was intended primarily for operation from grass strips, and tricycle landing gear was chosen as being more rational for a generation of amateur pilots who had received their initial flight training on aircraft equipped with landing gear of this configuration. Stressed to +6g and −3g, the Scamp can be used for limited aerobatics; and emphasis has been placed on simple construction techniques to make it an easy project for the homebuilder.

Plans and kits of parts, except for the Volkswagen engine, are available to amateur constructors. More than 500 sets of plans had been sold by early 1976. Four Scamps were then flying, and a further 18 were under construction from Aerosport kits

For details: Box 278, Holly Springs, North Carolina 27540, USA.

(USA)

AEROSPORT WOODY PUSHER

Two-seat light monoplane

Power plant: One 56 kW (75 hp) Continental flat-four engine. Provision for other engines in the 48.5-63.5 kW (65-85 hp) range
Wing span: 8.84 m (29 ft 0 in)
Wing area, gross: 12.07 m² (130 sq ft)
Length overall: 6.22 m (20 ft 5 in)
Height overall: 2.13 m (7 ft 0 in)
Weight empty: 285 kg (630 lb)
Max T-O weight: 522 kg (1,150 lb)
Max level speed at S/L: 85 knots (158 km/h; 98 mph)
Cruising speed: 76 knots (140 km/h; 87 mph)
Max rate of climb at S/L: 183 m (600 ft)/min
Endurance with max fuel: 2 hr 30 min

Accommodation: Two seats in tandem in open cockpits
Construction: Braced wooden wings, with metal leading-edge and fabric covering overall. Welded steel tube fuselage structure, fabric covered. Braced tail unit. Non-retractable landing gear

History: The prototype Woody Pusher was designed originally with a fuselage of wooden construction, plywood covered, with fabric covering overall, and was powered by a 48.5 kW (65 hp) Lycoming engine. Mr Woods, the designer and builder, subsequently redesigned the fuselage and landing gear and increased the engine power.
Several hundred sets of construction plans for the Woody Pusher have been sold; at least 27 aircraft have been completed and flown

For details: Box 278, Holly Springs, North Carolina 27540, USA.

Two-seat light monoplane

Power plant: One 67 kW (90 hp) Continental C90-14F flat-four engine
Wing span: 8.94 m (29 ft 4 in)
Wing area, gross: 11.20 m² (120.5 sq ft)
Length overall: 7.90 m (25 ft 11 in)
Weight empty: 524 kg (1,155 lb)
Max T-O weight: 728 kg (1,605 lb)
Max level speed: 105 knots (195 km/h; 121 mph)
Normal cruising speed: 86 knots (160 km/h; 99 mph)
Max rate of climb at S/L: 180 m (590 ft)/min
Service ceiling: 3,500 m (11,500 ft)
Range with max fuel: 323 nm (600 km; 373 miles)
Accommodation: Two seats in tandem under continuous transparent canopy, with separate side-hinged section over each seat
Construction: Wooden structure, covered with plywood. Non-retractable landing gear

History: Interest in the possibility of constructing a two-seat training aircraft at the École Nationale Supérieure d'Arts et Métiers at Cluny dates from 1965. Work on a prototype, designated AM-69, began in 1969, on the basis of incomplete plans of a tandem two-seat light aircraft known as the Gaucher RG-662 and design studies and experiments conducted at the school. Some 3,000 hours of new design and testing by a group of twelve students, and 4,000 hours of construction by ten other students, went into this all-wooden prototype, which flew for the first time on 6 May 1973.

It was certificated by the CNRA in July 1973, and was placed subsequently at the disposal of members of the Aero Club of Issoudun. The designers are working on an all-metal version, with larger vertical tail surfaces, a moulded canopy, revised engine cowling and other changes. Plans of this version are available to amateur constructors through the RSA

For details: RSA, 39 rue Sauffroy, 75017-Paris, France.

(USA)

Two-seat light amphibian

Data: Original 74.5 kW (100 hp) version
Power plant: One 74.5 kW (100 hp) Continental O-200 flat-four engine
Wing span: 11.00 m (36 ft 1 in)
Length overall: 7.16 m (23 ft 6 in)
Height overall: 2.44 m (8 ft 0 in)
Weight empty: 468 kg (1,032 lb)
Max T-O weight: 680 kg (1,500 lb)
Max cruising speed: 74 knots (136 km/h; 85 mph)
Max rate of climb at S/L: 150-180 m (500-600 ft)/min
Service ceiling: 3,050 m (10,000 ft)
Accommodation: Two seats side by side in enclosed cabin
Construction: Standard Piper Cub wing. Stabilising floats constructed from mahogany wood and plywood, coated with glassfibre. Wooden fuselage structure, covered with plywood and coated with glassfibre. Retractable landing gear

History: This aircraft, designed and built by Earl Anderson (a Boeing 747 captain), took nine years to complete at a cost of around $5,500. The first flight was made on 24 April 1969. After a time, Mr Anderson replaced the original 74.5 kW (100 hp) engine (as described above) by an 86 kW (115 hp) Lycoming O-235-C1 driving a Sensenich M76AM-4-44 propeller. With this power plant the Kingfisher has an empty weight of 495 kg (1,092 lb), a max T-O weight of 725 kg (1,600 lb) and improved performance. By January 1975 the prototype had accumulated more than 600 flying hours.

Plans available to amateur constructors cover the increase in weight. The Kingfisher was designed originally to accept alternative power plants up to a maximum of 140 hp, but on the basis of experience with the 115 hp Lycoming, Mr Anderson is discouraging homebuilders from installing more powerful engines.

Anderson Aircraft Corporation has been formed to market plans of the Kingfisher. By January 1976 well over 200 sets of plans had been sold, and more than 100 Kingfishers were under construction in the USA, Canada, Mexico, Sweden, Germany and Panama. At least ten are known to be flying

For details: PO Box 422, Raymond, Maine 04071, USA.

Single-seat fully-aerobatic light biplane

Data: Performance figures for prototype
Power plant: Prototype has one 74.5 kW (100 hp) Rolls-Royce Continental O-200-A flat-four engine. Provision for other engines, including Volkswagen conversions
Wing span: upper, 5.34 m (17 ft 7 in)
lower, 5.14 m (16 ft 11 in)
Wing area, gross: 8.3 m² (90 sq ft)
Length overall: 4.60 m (15 ft 0 in)
Max T-O weight: 375 kg (827 lb)
Max level speed: 122 knots (225 km/h; 140 mph)
Max cruising speed: 104 knots (193 km/h; 120 mph)
Max rate of climb at S/L: 600 m (2,000 ft)/min
Range with standard fuel: 152 nm (280 km; 175 miles)
Accommodation: Single seat in open cockpit
Construction: Braced wings of alternative all-metal or all-wood construction, the latter covered with heavy plywood. Pop-riveted ailerons, of simplified sheet metal construction, on lower wings only. Provision for fitting detachable plastics wingtips. Sheet metal fuselage structure, with turtleback of either metal or reinforced plastics. Tail unit of pop-riveted sheet metal construction. Non-retractable landing gear

History: An early design by Mr Bjorn Andreasson was the BA-4 biplane. This was subsequently modernised by him for members of the Swedish branch of the Experimental Aircraft Association, and a prototype was built by apprentices of the MFI apprentice school as part of their training programme. To distinguish this aircraft from the original BA-4, it is designated BA-4B.
World commercial manufacturing rights in the BA-4B are held by Mr P.J.C. Phillips of Midhurst, Sussex, England. The aircraft is being built in small numbers in the UK by Crosby Aviation Ltd, which also markets plans and kits for amateur constructors wishing to build their own aircraft. Plans for homebuilders also continue to be available from Mr Andreasson

For details: Mr B. Andreasson, c/o Saab-Scania, Box 463, S-201 24, Malmö 1, Sweden; Crosby Aviation Ltd, Archery House, Leycester Road, Knutsford, Cheshire, England.

Two-seat light sporting monoplane

Power plant: One 93 kW (125 hp) Lycoming O-290-G (GPU) flat-four engine in prototype. Design suitable for other engines in the 56-93 kW (75-125 hp) range
Wing span: 9.25 m (30 ft 4 in)
Wing area, gross: 12.8 m² (138 sq ft)
Length overall: 6.32 m (20 ft 9 in)
Height overall: 2.44 m (8 ft 0 in)
Weight empty: 407 kg (898 lb)
Max T-O weight: 680 kg (1,500 lb)
Max level speed at S/L: 126 knots (233 km/h; 145 mph)
Max cruising speed at S/L: 122 knots (225 km/h; 140 mph)
Max rate of climb at S/L: 610 m (2,000 ft)/min
Service ceiling: 5,180 m (17,000 ft)
Range with max fuel: 260 nm (482 km; 300 miles)
Accommodation: Two seats in tandem in open cockpits
Construction: Braced parasol wing of composite wood and steel tube structure, fabric covered. Welded steel tube Warren truss fuselage structure, fabric covered. Braced steel tube tail unit, fabric covered. Non-retractable landing gear

History: Mr Gerald Bakeng designed and built the prototype of this high-performance aircraft, which received the EAA's 'Outstanding New Design' and 'Design Improvement' awards in 1971. It was followed in 1972 by a tandem two-seat biplane known as the Bakeng Double Duce, which can be fitted with almost any engine in the 93-164 kW (125-220 hp) range.
Design and construction of the original Duce began in October 1969; it was completed six months later at a cost of approximately $1,500. The first flight was made on 2 April 1970.
Plans of the Duce and Double Duce are available to amateur constructors, and more than 200 sets of drawings of the Duce have been sold

For details: 19025 92nd W, Edmonds, Washington 98020, USA.

(USA)

BARNETT J-3M and J-4B

Single-seat light autogyros

Data: J-4B, except where indicated
Power plant: One 48.5 kW (65 hp) Continental A65 flat-four engine in J-3M. One 63.5 kW (85 hp) Continental C85 flat-four in J-4B
Rotor diameter, both versions: 7.01 m (23 ft 0 in)
Length overall: 3.71 m (12 ft 2 in)
Height overall: 2.34 m (7 ft 8 in)
Weight empty: 200 kg (441 lb)
Max T-O weight: 340 kg (750 lb)
Max level speed: 100 knots (185 km/h; 115 mph)
Cruising speed: 78 knots (145 km/h; 90 mph)
Max rate of climb at S/L: 213 m (700 ft)/min
Service ceiling: 4,265 m (14,000 ft)
Range: 217 nm (402 km; 250 miles)
Accommodation: Single seat in open or fully enclosed cockpit. Moulded Plexiglas windscreen; optional cockpit canopy

Construction: Rotor blades of spruce with single internal steel spar and glassfibre covering. All metal fuselage structure, with glassfibre streamlined nacelle. Tail unit of steel tube construction, fabric covered. Non-retractable landing gear

History: The Barnett Rotorcraft Company designed and built prototypes of these two generally-similar ultra-light gyroplanes. The basic differences between the J-3M and J-4B lie in the power plants used and in the degree of skill needed to construct them. Plans, materials and kits are available to amateur constructors.
The J-3M is the utility model, with a flat-sided fabric-covered cabin enclosure and powered by a 48.5 kW (65 hp) Continental A65 engine; the J-4B is a higher-performance version with 63.5 kW (85 hp) Continental C85 engine and streamlined glassfibre nacelle, as described above

For details: 4307 Olivehurst Avenue, Olivehurst, California 95961, USA.

J-4B version

Two/four-seat sporting and utility monoplane

Power plant: One 80.5 kW (108 hp) Lycoming O-235-C1 flat-four engine in two-seat version. Alternative engines for four-seat version include the 112 kW (150 hp) Lycoming O-320 and 134 kW (180 hp) Lycoming O-360, or a 149 kW (200 hp) engine.
Wing span: 7.80 m (25 ft 7 in)
Wing area, gross: 9.51 m² (102.33 sq ft)
Length overall: 6.52 m (21 ft 4½ in)
Width, wings folded: 2.20 m (7 ft 2¾ in)
Height overall: 2.20 m (7 ft 2¾ in)
Weight empty, two-seat version: 435 kg (960 lb)
Weight empty, 149 kW (200 hp) version: 510 kg (1,125 lb)
Max T-O weight, two-seat version: 725 kg (1,600 lb)
Max T-O weight, four-seat version: 907 kg (2,000 lb)
Max level speed at S/L, two-seat version: 135 knots (251 km/h; 156 mph)
Max level speed at S/L, 149 kW (200 hp) version: 176 knots (327 km/h; 203 mph)
Cruising speed (75% power), two-seat version: 126 knots (233 km/h; 145 mph)
Cruising speed (75% power), 149 kW (200 hp) version: 167 knots (309 km/h; 192 mph)
Max rate of climb at S/L, two-seat version: 274 m (900 ft)/min
Max rate of climb at S/L, 149 kW (200 hp) version: 518 m (1,700 ft)/min
Max range, 45 min reserve, all versions: 781 nm (1,448 km; 900 miles)
Accommodation: Two or four seats, in pairs, in enclosed cabin
Construction: Wing structure of glassfibre 'panel ribs' slid over extruded aluminium tubular spar, which fits over centre-section tube. Fuselage is a metal structure with aluminium or glassfibre skin. All-metal tail unit with aluminium skin. Non-retractable landing gear

History: Mr James R. Bede formed Bede Aircraft Inc to undertake production of plans and kits of parts for amateur construction of his BD-4 light aircraft. This can be built as a two- or four-seater, with various engines as listed above. By 1976 well over 2,000 sets of plans for the BD-4 had been sold; 736 aircraft were known to have flown. At least five have non-standard tailwheel-type landing gear

For details: Newton Municipal Airport, PO Box 706, Newton, Kansas 67114, USA.

Single-seat lightweight monoplanes

Data: BD-5G
Power plant: One 52 kW (70 hp) Xenoah three-cylinder two-stroke engine
Wing span: 5.18 m (17 ft 0 in)
Wing area, gross: 3.53 m² (38.0 sq ft)
Length overall, excl nose probe: 4.05 m (13 ft 3½ in)
Height overall: 1.28 m (4 ft 2½ in)
Weight empty: 186 kg (410 lb)
Max T-O weight: 385 kg (850 lb)
Max level speed at S/L: 200 knots (370 km/h; 230 mph)
Cruising speed at 2,285 m (7,500 ft): 182 knots (338 km/h; 210 mph)
Max rate of climb at S/L: 533 m (1,750 ft)/min
Service ceiling: 5,730 m (18,800 ft)
Range (75% power): 981 nm (1,818 km; 1,130 miles)
G limit: ± 6
Accommodation: Single seat under upward-opening transparent canopy. Cockpit heated and ventilated
Construction: Light alloy structure. Retractable landing gear

History: Design of this unusual sporting monoplane began in February 1967. Construction of the prototype was started in December 1970, and it made its first flight on 12 September 1971. Several versions have since appeared. The original prototype, designated BD-5A, had a wing span of 4.37 m (14 ft 4 in), was powered by a 30 kW (40 hp) Kiekhaefer Aeromarine two-cylinder two-stroke engine and had a 'butterfly' tail unit. A version was then produced with increased wing span and was designated BD-5B. As a result of early flight tests, the 'butterfly' tail unit was replaced by a conventional fin and rudder, with an all-moving horizontal 'stabilator' on the lower portion of the rear fuselage; in early 1974 Bede Aircraft decided to discontinue the short-span wing and the 30 kW (40 hp) engine. The designation BD-5B now refers to the basic version with 52 kW (70 hp) engine. The BD-5D is a factory-built version of the same model, and the BD-5S is a sailplane version. The latest, improved version is the BD-5G (as above) with a new wing section. It is fully aerobatic and includes several refinements. Yet another variant is the BD-5J, powered by a 0.90 kN (202 lb st) Microturbo TRS 18 turbojet engine, which gives it a maximum speed of 240 knots (444 km/h; 276 mph)

For details: Newton Municipal Airport, PO Box 706, Newton, Kansas 67114, USA.

BD-5J version

Single-seat lightweight sporting monoplane

Power plant: One 41 kW (55 hp) Hirth flat-two engine in prototype
Wing span: 6.55 m (21 ft 6 in)
Wing area, gross: 5.16 m² (55.5 sq ft)
Length overall: 5.11 m (16 ft 9 in)
Height overall: 1.98 m (6 ft 6 in)
Weight empty: 170 kg (375 lb)
Max T-O weight: 295 kg (650 lb)
Max level speed at S/L: over 122 knots (225 km/h; 140 mph)
Cruising speed at 2,285 m (7,500 ft): over 122 knots (225 km/h; 140 mph)
Max rate of climb at S/L: 274 m (900 ft)/min
Service ceiling: 4,265 m (14,000 ft)

Range (75% power) with 30 min reserve: 390 nm (724 km: 450 miles)
Accommodation: Single seat in enclosed cabin. Baggage space aft of seat
Construction: Similar to Bede BD-4, *which see*

History: The BD-6 is basically a single-seat development of the BD-4, with reduced overall dimensions and power. Although the prototype has flown, pressure of work on the BD-5D and BD-5J programmes has prevented further development of the BD-6, which is to be evaluated with both the 52 kW (70 hp) Xenoah and the 48.5 kW (65 hp) Continental engine

For details: Newton Municipal Airport, PO Box 706, Newton, Kansas 67114, USA.

Single-seat sporting monoplane

Power plant: One 52 kW (70 hp) Volkswagen 1,641 cc modified motor car engine in prototype. Design will accept engines of 37.25-74.5 kW (50-100 hp)
Wing span: 7.62 m (25 ft 0 in)
Length overall: 4.98 m (16 ft 4 in)
Height overall: 1.83 m (6 ft 0 in)
Weight empty: 274 kg (603 lb)
Max T-O weight: 420 kg (925 lb)
Max level speed at S/L: 135 knots (251 km/h; 156 mph)
Cruising speed: 104 knots (193 km/h; 120 mph)
Max rate of climb at S/L: 610 m (2,000 ft)/min
Range: 520 nm (965 km; 600 miles)

Accommodation: Single seat in open cockpit
Construction: Braced parasol wing of wooden construction, Dacron covered. Welded steel tube fuselage with Dacron covering. Wooden tail unit with foam filling, covered in plywood. Non-retractable landing gear

History: Mr G. Beets of Riverside, California, designed and built this lightweight sporting aircraft at a cost of approximately $2,500. Construction of the prototype occupied two years and the first flight was made on 25 July 1973. Plans for the G/B Special, kits of components and materials are available from Stolp Starduster Corporation

For details: 4301 Twining, Riverside, California 92509, USA.

BENSEN MODEL B-8 GYRO-GLIDER

Single-seat or two-seat unpowered rotor kite

Power plant: None
Rotor diameter: 6.10 m (20 ft 0 in)
Length of fuselage: 3.45 m (11 ft 4 in)
Height overall: 1.90 m (6 ft 3 in)
Minimum level flight speed: 16.5 knots (30.5 km/h; 19 mph)
Accommodation: Single seat or two seats in open position
Construction: Metal construction. Laminated plywood rotor. Non-retractable landing gear

History: The Gyro-Glider is an unpowered rotor kite which can be towed behind even a small motor car and has achieved free gliding with the towline released. It is available either as a complete aircraft or as a kit of parts for amateur construction. Alternatively, would-be constructors can purchase a set of plans, with building and flying instructions. No pilot's licence is required to fly it in the United States, and many hundreds of kits and plans have been sold.

The Model B-8 followed the original Model B-7 Gyro-Glider, and is offered as either a single- or side by side two-seater, the latter version being suitable for use as a pilot trainer.

The Model B-8 consists basically of an inverted square-section tubular aluminium T-frame structure, of which the forward arm supports the lightweight seat, towing arm, rudder bar and nosewheel. The rear arm supports a large stabilising fin and rudder, with the main landing gear wheels carried on a tubular axle near the junction of the T-frame. The free-turning two-blade rotor is universally-mounted at the top of the T-frame, and is normally tilted directly by a hanging-stick to control direction of flight, although a floor-type control column is optional. A movable rudder with pedal controls is standard

For details: PO Box 31047, Raleigh-Durham Airport, Raleigh, NC 27612, USA.

(USA)

BENSEN MODEL B-8M GYRO-COPTER

Single-seat light autogyro

Power plant: One 53.5 kW (72 hp) McCulloch Model 4318E flat-four two-stroke engine, or a 67 kW (90 hp) McCulloch 4318G or 47.5 kW (64 hp) Volkswagen 1,600 cc engine
Rotor diameter: 6.10 m (20 ft 0 in)
Length of fuselage: 3.45 m (11 ft 4 in)
Height overall: 1.90 m (6 ft 3 in)
Weight empty: 112 kg (247 lb)
Max T-O weight: 227 kg (500 lb)
Max level speed at S/L: 74 knots (137 km/h; 85 mph)
Max cruising speed at S/L: 52 knots (96.5 km/h; 60 mph)
Max rate of climb at S/L: 305 m (1,000 ft)/min
Service ceiling: 3,800 m (12,500 ft)
Normal range: 86 nm (160 km; 100 miles)
Accommodation: Single seat in open position
Construction: Metal fuselage structure. Fin and rudder of plywood (all-metal surfaces optional). Laminated plywood rotor (all-metal rotor optional). Non-retractable landing gear

History: First flown on 6 December 1955, the Gyro-Copter is a powered autogyro conversion of the Gyro-Glider, designed for home construction from kits or plans. When fitted with floats it is known as the Hydro-Copter.

The current B-8M version of the Gyro-Copter has a more powerful engine than the original B-7M, and can be equipped with an optional mechanical rotor drive. Other items available optionally include a 67 kW (90 hp) engine, a larger diameter rotor, an offset gimbal rotor head, a floor-type control column, dual ignition, nosewheel arrester and Bensen-manufactured pontoons.

The prototype Model B-8M first flew on 8 July 1957, and the first production model on 9 October 1957. It is fully roadable.

Derivatives are the Model B-8V, which is basically a B-8M powered by a 1,600 cc Volkswagen engine; the Super Bug which is an advanced version of the standard B-8M with a twin-engine installation to spin up the rotor prior to take-off; and the B-8H Hovering Gyro-Copter

For details: PO Box 31047, Raleigh-Durham Airport, Raleigh, NC 27612, USA.

B-8V Gyro-Copter

(France)

BESNEUX P.70B and POTTIER P.70S

Single-seat sporting monoplanes

Data: Pottier P.70S
Power plant: One Volkswagen motor car engine, modified to give 30-37.25 kW (40-50 hp)
Wing span: 5.90 m (19 ft 4½ in)
Wing area, gross: 7.20 m² (77.5 sq ft)
Length overall: 5.00 m (16 ft 4¾ in)
Weight empty: 180 kg (397 lb)
Max T-O weight: 290 kg (639 lb)
Max level speed at S/L: 97 knots (180 km/h; 112 mph)
Max cruising speed at S/L: 89 knots (165 km/h; 103 mph)
Max rate of climb at S/L: 300 m (985 ft)/min
Service ceiling: 4,500 m (14,775 ft)
Range with max fuel: 269 nm (500 km; 310 miles)
Accommodation: Single seat in enclosed cockpit

Construction: All-metal structure. Non-retractable landing gear

History: The P.70S is a small sporting aircraft derived from the P.70B, which was designed by M Jean Pottier and built by M Alain Besneux. Construction of the P.70B began in February 1972, and it flew for the first time on 19 July 1974. In its original form, with enclosed cockpit and a 30 kW (40 hp) Volkswagen engine, it had been exhibited at the 1973 Paris Air Show under the auspices of the RSA.
Design of the P.70S was started in January 1974, and twelve examples were known to be under construction by amateurs in early 1976, of which a few should have flown later in that year. Major changes in the P.70S, compared with the P.70B, include an increased wing span and installation of a tricycle landing gear

For details: 4 rue Emilio Castelar, 75012-Paris, France.

Besneux P.70B

Ultra-lightweight sporting monoplane

Power plant: One 11 kW (15 hp) Tally Aircraft M.C.101 DT single-cylinder two-stroke engine
Wing span: 10.36 m (34 ft 0 in)
Wing area, gross: 13.42 m² (144.5 sq ft)
Length overall: 6.10 m (20 ft 0 in)
Height overall: 2.18 m (7 ft 2 in)
Weight empty: 45 kg (100 lb)
Max T-O weight: 159 kg (350 lb)
Max level speed at S/L: 52 knots (97 km/h; 60 mph)
Max cruising speed at 1,980 m (6,500 ft): 47 knots (87 km/h; 54 mph)
Max rate of climb at S/L: 107 m (350 ft)/min
Service ceiling: 3,810 m (12,500 ft)
Range with max fuel: 174 nm (322 km; 200 miles)
Accommodation: Exposed seat with harness, adjustable to allow the pilot to fly the aircraft in an upright or semi-reclining position
Construction: Composite wing structure with wooden spar, wooden ribs, leading-edge D cell of reinforced expanded synthetic foam and aircraft Monokote covering. Three-part fuselage struc-ture; forward portion of riveted semi-monocoque light alloy, centre section of wood, and tapered plywood monocoque aft section. Non-retractable landing gear

History: Birdman Aircraft Inc designed the TL-1 with the aim of producing a strong, lightweight and inexpensive aircraft that could be assembled easily by a novice builder. In achieving this aim, it introduced some unusual ideas and materials. For example, the covering consists of a bi-axially oriented synthetic film known as Monokote, and this offers the key to the combination of light weight and strength.
Design of what qualified as the world's lightest powered aircraft began in 1969. The first flight was recorded six years later, on 25 January 1975, after considerable structural research and testing. The company is marketing the aircraft in kit form, with all materials, components, engine and accessories provided, together with plans and a builder's manual. By February 1976 over 200 kits were under construction

For details: 480 Midway (Airport), Daytona Beach, Florida 32014, USA.

Single-seat or two-seat light monoplane

Data: Original single-seat Fly Baby 1A
Power plant: One 63.5 kW (85 hp) Continental C75 flat-four engine
Wing span: 8.53 m (28 ft 0 in)
Length overall: 5.64 m (18 ft 6 in)
Height, wings folded: 1.98 m (6 ft 6 in)
Weight empty: 274 kg (605 lb)
Max T-O weight: 419 kg (924 lb)
Max level speed at S/L: over 104 knots (193 km/h; 120 mph)
Cruising speed: 91-96 knots (169-177 km/h; 105-110 mph)
Max rate of climb at S/L: 335 m (1,100 ft)/min
Range with max fuel: 277 nm (515 km; 320 miles)
Accommodation: Single seat in open or enclosed cockpit. Baggage in underfuselage 'tank'
Construction: Braced wings of wooden construction, covered with Dacron fabric and finished with two coats of nitrate dope and one coat of automotive enamel. Conventional plywood-covered wooden fuselage. Braced wooden tail unit, fabric covered. Non-retractable landing gear

History: The prototype Fly Baby monoplane was produced to compete in an EAA design contest, organised to encourage the development of a simple, low-cost, easy-to-fly aircraft that could be built by inexperienced amateurs for recreational flying. It was built in 720 working hours, at a cost of $1,050, and flew for the first time on 27 July 1960. It eventually won the contest. Following a crash in April 1962, when a pilot borrowed the Fly Baby and became lost in mountain country in bad weather, an entirely new fuselage was built. This is slightly longer than the original, with minor structural improvements. In addition, the original Continental A65 engine was replaced by the C75.

Home construction plans are available, and 3,725 sets had been sold by May 1976. Construction of well over 670 Fly Babies is known to have been undertaken, of which more than 165 have flown.

The Fly Baby monoplane has been tested as a twin-float seaplane. Following repeated requests, Mr Peter Bowers amended his plans during 1973 to allow for the construction of a two-seat version of the Fly-Baby. Changes include a wider (0.97 m; 3 ft 2 in) fuselage, insertion of a 1.52 m (5 ft 0 in) span wing centre-section to support a shock-absorbing landing gear, use of heavier flying wires, and recommended use of an engine in the 63.5-80.5 kW (85-108 hp) range

For details: 10458 16th Avenue South, Seattle, Washington 98168, USA.

Single-seat light biplane

Power plant: One 63.5 kW (85 hp) Continental C85 flat-four engine
Wing span: 6.71 m (22 ft 0 in)
Wing area, gross: 13.94 m² (150 sq ft)
Length overall: 5.64 m (18 ft 6 in)
Height overall: 2.08 m (6 ft 10 in)
Weight empty: 295 kg (651 lb)
Max T-O weight: 440 kg (972 lb)
Cruising speed: 75.5 knots (140 km/h; 87 mph)
Max rate of climb at S/L: 267 m (875 ft)/min
Range: approx 277 nm (515 km; 320 miles)
Accommodation: Single seat in open cockpit
Construction: Wooden wing structure, Dacron covered. Conventional plywood-covered wooden fuselage. Wooden tail unit, fabric covered. Non-retractable landing gear

History: During 1968 Mr Bowers designed and built a set of interchangeable biplane wings for the original prototype Fly Baby; with these fitted, it flew for the first time on 27 March 1969.

The biplane wings have the same aerofoil section and incidence as those of the monoplane version, but the rib webs are made of thinner plywood and the wingtip bows are formed from aluminium tube instead of laminated wood strips. The lightweight construction limits weight increase to only 21 kg (46 lb), for an increase of 2.79 m² (30 sq ft) in wing area. Ailerons are fitted to the lower wings only. Changeover from monoplane to biplane configuration can be accomplished by two people in approximately one hour

For details: 10458 16th Avenue South, Seattle, Washington 98168, USA.

Two-seat sporting monoplane

Power plant: One 93 kW (125 hp) Lycoming O-290-G (GPU) flat-four engine
Wing span: 10.06 m (33 ft 0 in)
Wing area, gross: 13.9 m² (150 sq ft)
Length overall: 6.55 m (21 ft 6 in)
Weight empty: 544 kg (1,200 lb)
Max T-O weight: 839 kg (1,850 lb)
Max level speed: 122 knots (225 km/h; 140 mph)
Cruising speed: 109 knots (203 km/h; 126 mph)
Max rate of climb at S/L: 290 m (950 ft)/min
Service ceiling: 4,570 m (15,000 ft)
Range with max fuel: 434 nm (804 km; 500 miles)
Accommodation: Two seats side by side under transparent canopy. Dual controls. Stowage for 45 kg (100 lb) of baggage under and aft of seats

Construction: Three-piece single-spar wing structure. The spar has spruce flanges and plywood webs. The leading-edge torsion box is a sandwich of two sheets of aluminium with glassfibre cloth between, epoxy-cemented together and formed over plywood nose ribs. The ribs aft of the spar are cut from plywood. Wing is Dacron-covered. Wooden tail unit, Dacron covered. Non-retractable landing gear

History: Mr Peter Bowers designed and built the prototype of this two-seat light aircraft, which first flew on 2 July 1975. Known as the Namu II, it is named after Seattle's famous captive whale – reflecting its bulky appearance by comparison with the Fly Baby. Another Namu II, with a different canopy, has been completed by Richard Lowe and Tom Godbey of Seattle

For details: 10458 16th Avenue South, Seattle, Washington 98168, USA.

Three-seat parasol-wing monoplane

Data: Prototype
Power plant: One 67 kW (90 hp) Continental C90-8F-P flat-four engine
Wing span: 10.06 m (33 ft 0 in)
Wing area, gross: 15.3 m² (165 sq ft)
Length overall: 6.86 m (22 ft 6 in)
Height overall: 2.59 m (8 ft 6 in)
Weight empty: 317 kg (700 lb)
Max T-O weight: 544 kg (1,200 lb)
Never-exceed speed: 91 knots (168 km/h; 105 mph)
Cruising speed (70% power): 65 knots (121 km/h; 75 mph)
Service ceiling: 4,575 m (15,000 ft)
Range with max fuel: 217 nm (402 km; 250 miles)
Accommodation: Three seats in tandem; pilot on front seat and two passengers on bench seat to the rear
Construction: Braced Piper PA-12 wing. Welded steel tube fuselage structure, without covering. Braced steel tube tail unit, fabric covered. Non-retractable landing gear

History: Three professional pilots designed and built the prototype of this aptly-named light aircraft, the designation RLU being made up of the initial letters of their surnames. Well over 500 sets of plans have been sold, and many Breezys are flying, including examples built in Australia, Canada and South Africa.

Described as being of vintage configuration with all modern facilities, such as full radio, instruments and hydraulic brakes, the prototype first flew on 7 August 1964, having taken six months to built at a cost of $3,400. The first Breezy to be built from the published plans differed from the prototype in having only two seats. Other modifications have been made to subsequent aircraft; one, built by Mr R Fabian, utilises the wing, tail unit, wheels and fairings, wheel brakes and seats of a Cessna Model 172, and is powered by a 108 kW (145 hp) Continental O-300-D engine

For details: Charles B Roloff, 8025 West 90th Street, Hickory Hills, Illinois 60457, USA.

RLU-1 with a Lycoming O-290-G engine

Two-seat sporting monoplane

Data: Latest, modified form
Power plant: One 283 kW (380 hp) Lycoming TIO-541-A engine
Wing span: 7.21 m (23 ft 8 in)
Wing area, gross: 8.95 m² (96.3 sq ft)
Length overall: 6.94 m (22 ft 9 in)
Height overall: 2.69 m (8 ft 10 in)
Weight empty (approx): over 975 kg (2,149 lb)
Max T-O weight (approx): over 1,357 kg (2,993 lb)
Max cruising speed (70% power) at 7,300 m (24,000 ft), estimated: over 278 knots (515 km/h; 320 mph)
Max rate of climb at S/L: over 915 m (3,000 ft)/min
Range (approx): 542 nm (1,005 km; 625 miles)
Accommodation: Two seats in tandem beneath transparent individual canopies. Space for 18 kg (40 lb) of baggage aft of rear seat
Construction: All-metal construction. Retractable landing gear

History: Dr B.F. Brokaw, a former US Navy pilot, and Dr E. Jones combined their talents to design and build an aircraft which was claimed to be the fastest homebuilt in the world. Design emphasis was on evolving a high-speed all-weather two-seat homebuilt suitable for cross-country flying. Aerobatic potential was a secondary consideration, but the BJ-520 is stressed to ± 6 g for aerobatics and 9 g ultimate.

Design began in September 1966, and construction of the prototype started five months later. First flight of the BJ-520 was made on 18 November 1972, and during the Summer of 1973 work was carried out to clean up the airframe to achieve the full potential of the design. Further refinement of the aircraft was being undertaken in the mid-seventies and the modified BJ-520 was expected to fly again in 1977. Latest refinements include changes to the wings (span increased from 6.20 m; 20 ft 4 in) and power plant (the Avco Lycoming replacing the 212.5 kW (285 hp) Continental TSIO-520B turbocharged engine which gave the aircraft a max speed of 453 km/h; 282 mph).

Dr Brokaw has formed a company to market information and plans of the BJ-520 to amateur constructors. If there is sufficient demand, it is intended to supply certain components to simplify the task of the homebuilder

For details: 2625 Johnson Point, Leesburg, Florida 32748, USA.

(Switzerland)

BRÜGGER MB-2 COLIBRI 2

Single-seat light monoplane

Power plant: One 30 kW (40 hp) 1,600 cc Volkswagen engine
Wing span: 6.00 m (19 ft 8¼ in)
Wing area, gross: 8.20 m² (88.25 sq ft)
Length overall: 4.80 m (15 ft 9 in)
Height overall: 1.60 m (5 ft 3 in)
Weight empty: 215 kg (474 lb)
Max T-O weight: 330 kg (727 lb)
Max level speed at 4,000 m (13,125 ft): 97 knots (180 km/h; 111 mph)
Econ cruising speed (70% power), height as above: 86 knots (160 km/h; 99 mph)
Max rate of climb at S/L: 180 m (590 ft)/min
Service ceiling: 4,500 m (14,750 ft)

Range with max fuel: 270 nm (500 km; 310 miles)
Accommodation: Single seat under transparent canopy, with quarter-lights to rear
Construction: Wooden structure, plywood covered except for wings, which are fabric covered. Non-retractable landing gear

History: The Colibri 2 followed the Brügger Colibri 1 single-seat ultra-light aircraft which first flew on 30 October 1965. Design of the Colibri 2 began in January 1966. Construction was started a year later, and the first of two prototypes flew for the first time on 1 May 1970. By early 1976, about 65 Colibri 2s were under construction by amateur builders in Europe, and at least three others were flying

For details: 1751 Villarsel-le-Gibloux, Fribourg, Switzerland.

(USA)

BUSHBY/LONG MM-1 MIDGET MUSTANG

Single-seat fully-aerobatic sporting monoplane

landing gear

Data: MM-1-125
Power plant: One 101 kW (135 hp) Lycoming O-290-D2 flat-four piston engine (MM-1-85 is powered by 63.5 kW; 85 hp Continental C85-8FJ or -12 piston engine)
Wing span: 5.64 m (18 ft 6 in)
Wing area, gross: 6.32 m² (68 sq ft)
Length overall: 5.00 m (16 ft 5 in)
Height overall: 1.37 m (4 ft 6 in)
Weight empty: 268 kg (590 lb)
Max T-O and landing weight: 408 kg (900 lb)
Max level speed at S/L: 195 knots (362 km/h; 225 mph)
Max cruising speed at 2,440 m (8,000 ft): 187 knots (346 km/h; 215 mph)
Max rate of climb at S/L: 670 m (2,200 ft)/min
Service ceiling: 5,790 m (19,000 ft)
Range with max fuel: 325 nm (603 km; 375 miles)
Accommodation: Single seat under canopy hinged on starboard side. Space for 5.5 kg (12 lb) of baggage
Construction: All-metal construction. Usually non-retractable

History: Mr Robert Bushby, a research engineer with Sinclair Oil Co, built the first Midget Mustang, using drawings, jigs and certain components produced by the aircraft's designer, the late David Long. He has since produced the aircraft in kit form, and also offers sets of plans of the Midget Mustang to amateur constructors.

The original prototype was completed in 1948 by David Long, then chief engineer of the Piper company. He flew it in the National Air Races that year, and in 1949 was placed fourth in the Continental Trophy Race at Miami. Two basic versions have been developed by Robert Bushby: the MM-I-85, powered by a 63.5 kW (85 hp) Continental engine, which first flew on 9 September 1959, and the MM-1-125, powered by a 101 kW (135 hp) Lycoming engine, which first flew in July 1963. Ninety Midget Mustangs have been completed, with 800 more under construction throughout the world. Several of those now flying have a 112 kW (150 hp) Lycoming O-320 engine, providing a cruising speed of 234 knots (435 km/h; 270 mph) at 2,440 m (8,000 ft). Some have been fitted with retractable main landing gear

For details: Route 1, PO Box 13B, Minooka, Illinois 60447, USA.

Two-seat light monoplane

Power plant: Normally one 119 kW (160 hp) Lycoming O-320 flat-four piston engine
Wing span: 7.37 m (24 ft 2 in)
Wing area, gross: 9.02 m² (97.12 sq ft)
Length overall: 5.94 m (19 ft 6 in)
Height overall: 1.60 m (5 ft 3 in)
Weight empty: 420 kg (927 lb) with tailwheel landing gear
Normal max T-O and landing weight: 680 kg (1,500 lb)
Max level speed at S/L: 177 knots (328 km/h; 204 mph)
Max cruising speed at 2,285 m (7,500 ft): 175 knots (323 km/h; 201 mph)
Max rate of climb at S/L: 425 m (1,400 ft)/min
Service ceiling: 5,485 m (18,000 ft)
Range with standard fuel (75% power): 373 nm (692 km; 430 miles)
Accommodation: Two seats side by side under large rearward-sliding transparent canopy. Dual controls. Baggage space aft, with capacity of 34 kg (75 lb)
Construction: All-metal construction. Retractable or non-retractable landing gear

History: Design of this side-by-side two-seat derivative of the Midget Mustang was started in 1963. Construction of a prototype began in 1965, and it flew for the first time on 9 July 1966. During 1968 Mr Bushby designed an alternative non-retractable tricycle landing gear for the Mustang II, and amateur constructors have the option of either fixed or retractable gear. At least 700 Mustang IIs were being built by amateurs in 1976, at which time 40 were flying. At least one Mustang II has been fitted with a mechanically-actuated retractable main landing gear and other modifications. The M-II can also be operated as an aerobatic type, in what Bushby Aircraft calls the 'Sport' configuration. This is identical to the de luxe model, except that certain electrical items are deleted and the empty and T-O weights are 340/567 kg (750/1,250 lb) respectively.

For details: Route 1, PO Box 13B, Minooka, Illinois 60447, USA.

Mustang II with a 149 kW (200 hp) Lycoming IO-360-A1A engine

Single-seat racing monoplane

Data: Original Cassutt Special I, named *Jersey Skeeter*
Power plant: One 63.5 kW (85 hp) Continental C85-8F flat-four piston engine
Wing span: 4.54 m (14 ft 11 in)
Wing area, gross: 6.13 m² (66.0 sq ft)
Length overall: 4.88 m (16 ft 0 in)
Height overall: 1.30 m (4 ft 3 in)
Weight empty: 234 kg (516 lb)
Max T-O weight: 331 kg (730 lb)
Max level speed: 200 knots (370 km/h; 230 mph)
Max cruising speed: 165 knots (306 km/h; 190 mph)
Max rate of climb at S/L: 610 m (2,000 ft)/min
Endurance with max fuel: 3 hours
Accommodation: Single seat in enclosed cockpit
Construction: Wooden wing structure with plywood skin, fabric covered. Steel tube fuselage, tail unit and aileron structures, fabric covered. Non-retractable landing gear

History: While employed as an airline pilot, Capt Tom Cassutt designed and built in 1954 a small single-seat racing aircraft known as the Cassutt Special I (No 111), in which he won the 1958 National Air Racing Championships. In 1959, he completed a smaller aircraft on the same lines, known as the Cassutt Special II (No 11). Plans of both aircraft, and of a sporting version of No 111 with a larger cockpit, are available to amateur constructors. As a result, many Cassutt Specials are flying and under construction.

Airmark Ltd in the UK built a few slightly modified examples of the Cassutt Special I; these are known as Airmark/Cassutt 111Ms in Britain. First Cassutt Special to be completed in Australia flew for the first time in 1974, powered by a 74.5 kW (100 hp) Rolls-Royce Continental engine.

For details: 11718 Persuasion Drive, San Antonio, Texas 78216, USA.

(France)

Single-seat light monoplane

Data: YC-122
Power plant: One 71 kW (95 hp) Continental C90 or 74.5 kW (100 hp) Rolls-Royce Continental O-200-A engine. Alternative engines as listed below
Wing span: 6.70 m (22 ft 0 in)
Wing area, gross: 7.50 m² (80.7 sq ft)
Length overall: 5.85 m (19 ft 2¼ in)
Height overall: 2.40 m (7 ft 10½ in)
Weight empty: 313 kg (690 lb)
Max T-O weight: 460 kg (1,015 lb)
Max level speed at S/L (estimated): 146 knots (270 km/h; 168 mph)
Max cruising speed (70% power) estimated: 129 knots (240 km/h; 149 mph)
Max rate of climb at S/L: 420 m (1,380 ft)/min
Max range: 377 nm (700 km; 435 miles)
Accommodation: Single seat under large transparent rearward-sliding canopy. Baggage space aft of seat
Construction: Wooden structure, plywood covered. Non-

CHASLE YC-12 TOURBILLON (WHIRLWIND)

retractable landing gear

History: When M Yves Chasle designed the Tourbillon, its dimensions were governed by the maximum size that could be accommodated in his garage workshop. First flight was made on 9 October 1965. As a result of the flight tests leading to its restricted C of A, the height of the vertical tail surfaces was later increased slightly.
Plans for this aircraft are available to amateur constructors, and the Tourbillon can be built in a variety of forms, differing only in the type of engine fitted. YC-121 is the designation of the aircraft fitted with a 48.5 kW (65 hp) Continental A65 engine. The YC-122 is described above. The YC-123 has a 78.5 kW (105 hp) Potez 4E-20b engine. Its dimensions and weights are similar to those listed above, but it is the fastest version with a max level speed of 151 knots (280 km/h; 174 mph). Amateur construction of YC-12s has been undertaken in several countries, including France, Canada, the US, New Zealand and the UK

For details: Le Goya, rue de Traynes, 65-Tarbes, France; North America: E. Littner, 546 83rd Avenue, Laval-Chomedey, Quebec, Canada.

Single-seat lightweight sporting monoplane

Data: Performance figures with 1,600 cc engine
Power plant: One 48.5 kW (65 hp) modified Volkswagen 1,600 cc motor car engine. (Two aircraft fitted with 48.5 kW; 65 hp Continental engines)
Wing span: 7.32 m (24 ft 0 in)
Wing area, gross: 7.76 m² (83.5 sq ft)
Length overall: 4.98 m (16 ft 4 in)
Height overall: 1.80 m (5 ft 11 in)
Weight empty: 225 kg (497 lb)
Max T-O weight: 385 kg (850 lb)
Max level speed at 610 m (2,000 ft): 91 knots (169 km/h; 105 mph)
Max cruising speed at 610 m (2,000 ft): 78 knots (145 km/h; 90 mph)
Max rate of climb at S/L: 229 m (750 ft)/min
Service ceiling: 3,810 m (12,500 ft)
Range with max fuel, 20 min reserve: 260 nm (482 km, 300 miles)

Accommodation: Single seat in open cockpit. Transparent cockpit canopy optional. Baggage compartment aft of headrest
Construction: All-metal construction, with glassfibre wingtips. Non-retractable landing gear

History: Design of the Mini Coupe originated in June 1968, and construction of the first prototype began in July 1970. This aircraft made its first flight in September 1971 and FAA certification in the Experimental Category was awarded on 2 June 1972. Kits of components and materials, less engine, are available to amateur constructors. At least 156 sets of plans had been sold by early 1976, when 26 Mini Coupes were known to be flying.
Glassfibre wingtip extensions were added to the standard Mini Coupe in 1975, to increase the wing area. This improves the glide ratio, makes the aircraft more stable during banks, and has reduced stalling speed.

For details: PO Box 1, Hillsboro, Oregon 97123, USA.

Single-seat ultra-light monoplane

Power plant: Any suitable engine up to 56 kW (75 hp) and 72 kg (160 lb) weight
Wing span: 5.64 m (18 ft 6 in)
Wing area, gross: 6.36 m² (68.50 sq ft)
Length overall: 4.50 m (14 ft 9 in)
Max width, fuselage: 0.55 m (1 ft 9¾ in)
Height overall: 1.47 m (4 ft 10 in)
Weight empty: 183-190 kg (405-420 lb)
Max T-O weight (semi-aerobatic); 295 kg (650 lb)
Max level speed, with 36.5 kW (49 hp) engine, at 295 kg (650 lb) AUW: 117 knots (217 km/h; 135 mph)
Max cruising speed, engine and weight as above: 107 knots (198 km/h; 123 mph)
Typical rate of climb at S/L, engine and weight as above: 213-259 m (700-850 ft)/min
Service ceiling, engine and weight as above: 4,420 m (14,500 ft)

G **Limits:** ± 4.5
Accommodation: Single seat. Sliding canopy optional. Baggage locker behind seat
Construction: Wooden structure, plywood and fabric covered. Non-retractable landing gear

History: Mr Corby, a consultant aero engineer, has designed and is marketing plans for a single-seat ultra-light aircraft known as the Starlet. By March 1976 nine Starlets had been completed and a further 40 were known to be under construction in Australia, Tasmania and New Zealand, including a metal construction Starlet (usual structure of wood).

The first Starlet (VH-ULV) was built by a class of about ten members of the Latrobe Valley division of the Ultra-Light Aircraft Association, with Mr Erle Jones (Secretary and former President of the ULAA, Latrobe Valley Aero Club) test flying the aircraft and Mr John Brown acting as the instructor in building techniques.

For details: 86 Eton Street, Sutherland, NSW 2232, Australia.

(France)

CROSES EAC-3 POUPLUME

Single-seat ultra-light biplane

Data: First prototype, except where indicated
Power plant: One 7.8 kW (10.5 hp) Moto 232 cc two-stroke motor-cycle engine in prototype. Various other engines can be installed, including Volkswagen conversions
Wing span: forward 7.80 m (25 ft 7 in)
rear 7.00 m (23 ft 0 in)
Wing area, gross: 16.0 m² (172 sq ft)
Length overall: 3.00 m (9 ft 10 in)
Height overall: 1.80 m (5 ft 11 in)
Weight empty: 110-140 kg (243-310 lb)
Max T-O weight: 220-260 kg (485-573 lb)
Max level speed: 38 knots (70 km/h; 43.5 mph)
Max level speed, with 13.4 kW (18 hp) engine: 65 knots (120 km/h; 75 mph)

Econ cruising speed: 27 knots (50 km/h; 31 mph)
Take-off speed: 13.5 knots (25 km/h; 15.5 mph)
Accommodation: Single seat in open cockpit
Construction: Spruce wing structure and spruce fuselage, covered with okoumé ply. Non-retractable landing gear

History: As in the familiar Mignet Pou-du-Ciel designs, the Pouplume has a fixed rear wing and a pivoted forward wing, which dispenses with the need for ailerons and elevators. A conventional rudder is fitted, with a large tailwheel built into its lower edge.
The EAC-3-01 Pouplume took 600 hours to build, and flew for the first time in June 1961. It was followed in 1967 by a second prototype (EAC-3-02), with a 20 cm (8 in) longer fuselage. M Emilien Croses is offering sets of plans to amateur constructors, and several other examples of the Pouplume are flying

For details: Route de Davayé, 71-Charnay les Macon, France.

(France)

Two-seat light aircraft

Power plant: One 67 kW (90 hp) Continental flat-four engine
Wing span: forward 7.80 m (25 ft 7 in)
rear 7.00 m (22 ft 11½ in)
Wing area, gross: 16.0 m² (172 sq ft)
Length overall: 4.65 m (15 ft 3 in)
Weight empty: 290 kg (639 lb)
Max T-O weight: 550 kg (1,213 lb)
Max level speed at S/L: 115 knots (213 km/h; 132 mph)
Max cruising speed: 92 knots (170 km/h; 106 mph)
Min flying speed (aircraft will not stall): 22 knots (40 km/h; 25 mph)
Climb to 2,000 m (6,560 ft): 6 min 14 sec
Accommodation: Two seats side by side in enclosed cockpit
Construction: Wooden wing structure, with plywood leading-edge, overall fabric covering and some components of glassfibre.

CROSES EC-6 CRIQUET (LOCUST)

Wooden fuselage and tail unit structures, plywood covered. Glassfibre engine cowling. Non-retractable landing gear

History: This aircraft is a development of the earlier EC-1-02 of around 1960. Construction was started in March 1964 and the EC-6-01 flew for the first time on 6 July 1965.

In 1975, M Croses was completing the prototype of an all-plastics version of the Criquet. The fuselage, engine cowling, fin, wing spars, upper wing support struts and main landing gear legs are made from polyester, resin and glassfibre. The wing ribs and certain components are of Klégécel. Other parts are made from a balsa/glassfibre composite material.

Plans of the original wooden version of the Criquet are available to amateur constructors. It is hoped to make available later both plans and kits of the plastics version, with some 40% of the components finished and ready for assembly

For details: Route de Davayé, 71-Charnay les Macon, France.

(USA)

CVJETKOVIC CA-61/61R MINI ACE

Single-seat or two-seat light monoplane

Data: CA-61 prototype
Power plant: One 48.5 kW (65 hp) Continental A65 flat-four engine
Wing span: 8.38 m (27 ft 6 in)
Wing area, gross: 11.75 m² (126.5 sq ft)
Length overall: 5.77 m (18 ft 11 in)
Height overall (in flying position): 2.08 m (6 ft 10 in)
Weight empty: single-seat 275 kg (606 lb)
           two-seat   363 kg (800 lb)
Max T-O weight: single-seat 430 kg (950 lb)
           two-seat   590 kg (1,300 lb)
Max level speed at S/L: 104 knots (193 km/h; 120 mph)
Normal cruising speed: 87 knots (161 km/h; 100 mph)
Range with max fuel: single-seat 369 nm (685 km; 425 miles)
           two-seat   321 nm (595 km; 370 miles)
Accommodation: One or two seats in enclosed cockpit

Construction: Wooden structure, plywood covered except for wings, which are fabric covered. Non-retractable landing gear

History: After emigrating to the United States from Yugoslavia, Mr Anton Cvjetkovic began work, in May 1960, on the design of an improved version of the CA-51 light aircraft for which he had been responsible ten years earlier. Construction of the prototype, which he designated CA-61, was started in February 1961, and it flew for the first time in August 1962. Plans of both single-seat and two-seat versions of the CA-61 are available to amateur constructors, who can fit any Continental engine of between 48.5 and 63.5 kW (65 to 85 hp). Alternatively, the single-seater can be powered with a modified Volkswagen engine. Construction takes less than 1,000 hours. In 1973 the design was modified to allow the installation of retractable landing gear; when constructed in this form the aircraft is designated CA-61R. For numbers of plans sold, see CA-65 entry
For details: 624 Fowler Avenue, PO Box 323, Newbury Park, California 91320, USA.

CA-61R Mini Ace

Two-seat light monoplanes

Data: CA-65
Power plant: One 93 kW (125 hp) Lycoming O-290-G flat-four engine
Wing span: 7.62 m (25 ft 0 in)
Wing area, gross: 10.03 m² (108 sq ft)
Length overall: 5.79 m (19 ft 0 in)
Height overall (in flying position): 2.24 m (7 ft 4 in)
Weight empty: 408 kg (900 lb)
Max T-O weight: 680 kg (1,500 lb)
Max level speed: 139 knots (257 km/h; 160 mph)
Normal cruising speed: 117 knots (217 km/h; 135 mph)
Max rate of climb at S/L: 305 m (1,000 ft)/min
Service ceiling: 4,575 m (15,000 ft)
Range with max fuel: 434 nm (804 km; 500 miles)
Accommodation: Two seats side by side in enclosed cockpit, with dual controls.
Construction: All-wood structure, plywood covered except for ailerons, elevator and rudder which are fabric covered. Retractable landing gear

History: Design work on the CA-65 started in September 1963. Construction of the prototype began in March 1964 and was completed in 1965, the first flight taking place in July of that year. Plans are available to amateur constructors.

The CA-65 closely resembles the CA-61 in general appearance, but has a retractable landing gear and a more powerful engine. A folding-wing version was introduced during 1967.

The CA-65A is basically similar to the all-wood CA-65, but differs in having swept vertical tail surfaces and being of all-metal construction. It is designed for $+9g$ and $-6g$ ultimate loading, and can accommodate a Lycoming engine of between 80.5 and 112 kW (108-150 hp). Maximum speed is 151 knots (280 km/h; 174 mph) with a 112 kW (150 hp) engine.

By early 1976 a total of more than 300 sets of plans of the CA-61/CA-65 series of aircraft had been sold, and completed aircraft are flying in Canada, South Africa and the United States

For details: 624 Fowler Avenue, PO Box 323, Newbury Park, California 91320, USA.

CA-65

(USA)

D'APUZZO D-260 SENIOR AERO SPORT

Two-seat sporting biplane

Data: D-260 (3)
Power plant: One 194 kW (260 hp) Lycoming GO-435 flat-six engine
Wing span: 8.23 m (27 ft 0 in)
Wing area, gross: 17.2 m² (185 sq ft)
Length overall: 6.40 m (21 ft 0 in)
Height overall: 2.32 m (7 ft 7½ in)
Max T-O weight: 975 kg (2,150 lb)
Max level speed at 2,135 m (7,000 ft): 135 knots (250 km/h; 155 mph)
Max cruising speed at above height: 122 knots (225 km/h; 140 mph)
Max rate of climb at S/L: 610 m (2,000 ft)/min
Service ceiling: 6,100 m (20,000 ft)
Range with max fuel and max payload: 434 nm (805 km; 500 miles)
Accommodation: Two seats in tandem in open cockpits. Baggage space behind headrest
Construction: Composite wing structure, with wooden spars and metal ribs, fabric covered. Steel tube fuselage and tail unit, fabric covered except for aluminium alloy cowling panels forward of cockpit. Non-retractable landing gear

History: Mr Nicholas D'Apuzzo has designed several sporting aircraft for amateur construction, the best-known of which include the Denight Special midget racer and the PJ-260 single-seat aerobatic biplane, which were last described in the 1962-63 and 1974-75 editions of *Jane's All the World's Aircraft* respectively. The Senior Aero Sport is a two-seat version of the PJ-260. By 1976 a total of 28 PJ-260s and Senior Aero Sports were known to have been completed by amateur constructors in the United States, with a further 96 under construction.

There are five basic versions of the Senior Aero Sport, as follows: D-260 (1) with Lycoming O-435 engine; D-260 (2) first flown on 17 July 1965 with a 168 kW (225 hp) Continental E-185 engine; D-260 (3) as described above. First flown on 17 July 1965 with a GO-435-C2 engine; D-260 (4) with Ranger 6-440-C inverted in-line engine; D-260 (5) with 229 kW (300 hp) Lycoming R-680-E3 radial engine

For details: 1029 Blue Rock Lane, Blue Bell, Pennsylvania 19422, USA.

Two-seat light monoplane

Power plant: One 48.5 kW (65 hp) Continental A65-8 flat-four engine
Wing span: 5.86 m (19 ft 2¾ in)
Wing area, gross: 7.66 m² (82.5 sq ft)
Length overall: 5.44 m (17 ft 10¼ in)
Height overall: 1.65 m (5 ft 5 in)
Weight empty: 277 kg (610 lb)
Max T-O weight: 510 kg (1,125 lb)
Max level speed at S/L: 104 knots (193 km/h; 120 mph)
Cruising speed: 100 knots (185 km/h; 115 mph)
Range with max fuel: 390 nm (725 km; 450 miles)
Accommodation: Two seats side-by-side in fully enclosed cabin. Child's seat or baggage space at rear of cabin

Construction: All-metal construction. Non-retractable landing gear

History: This light aircraft was flown for the first time on 21 May 1966, after 18 months of spare-time work and an expenditure of $1,600. At the Experimental Aircraft Association's annual Fly-in a few weeks later, it gained awards for both the most outstanding design and the most popular aircraft. Plans are available to amateur constructors.

By early 1976 the prototype had flown a total of 860 hours, and the 20 DA-2As that were flying had accumulated approximately 4,000 flying hours. It is believed that about 100 more DA-2As are under construction

For details: PO Box 207, 405 North St Paul, Stanton, Texas 79782, USA.

(USA)

DAVIS DA-5A

Single-seat sporting monoplane

Power plant: One 48.5 kW (65 hp) Continental A65 flat-four engine
Wing span: 4.76 m (15 ft 7¼ in)
Wing area, gross: 5.31 m² (57.20 sq ft)
Length overall: 4.80 m (15 ft 9 in)
Height overall: 1.35 m (4 ft 5¼ in)
Weight empty: 208 kg (460 lb)
Max T-O weight: 351 kg (775 lb)
Max level speed at S/L: 139 knots (257 km/h; 160 mph)
Max cruising speed at S/L: 122 knots (225 km/h; 140 mph)
Max rate of climb at S/L: 244 m (800 ft)/min
Service ceiling: 4,420 m (14,500 ft)
Range with max fuel: 390 nm (724 km; 450 miles)

Accommodation: Single seat beneath hinged canopy
Construction: All-metal construction. Non-retractable landing gear

History: Design of this aircraft began in October 1972, but it was not until 4 May 1974 that Mr Leeon Davis and his son were able to begin construction of the prototype. It was intended originally to power the aircraft with a two-cylinder Franklin Sport 2 engine, but non-availability of this power plant brought a design change in mid-stream to utilise a Continental A65. Despite the extra work involved, the first flight was made on 22 July 1974. Plans are available to amateur constructors

For details: PO Box 207, 405 North St Paul, Stanton, Texas 79782, USA.

Single-seat sporting monoplane

Data: Prototype
Power plant: Prototype has one 48.5 kW (65 hp) Lycoming O-145-B2 flat-four engine (*see also History*)
Wing span: 6.21 m (20 ft 4½ in)
Wing area, gross: 5.95 m² (64 sq ft)
Length overall: 4.57 m (15 ft 0 in)
Height overall: 1.83 m (6 ft 0 in)
Weight empty: 238 kg (525 lb)
Max T-O weight: 405 kg (893 lb)
Max level speed at 1,525 m (5,000 ft): 127 knots (235 km/h; 146 mph)
Max cruising speed at above height: 114 knots (211 km/h; 131 mph)
Max rate of climb at S/L: 457 m (1,500 ft)/min
Service ceiling: 3,660 m (12,000 ft)
Range with max fuel, 45 min reserve: 477 nm (885 km; 550 miles)
Accommodation: Single seat in enclosed cockpit. Baggage space aft of pilot's seat. Cockpit heated and ventilated
Construction: All-metal construction, using a surplus military drop-tank as the basis of the fuselage. Non-retractable landing gear

History: Mr Richard Killingsworth designed and built this light aircraft, which he named the DSK-1 Hawk. Interest in the design was such that he formed DSK Airmotive Inc to market plans and partial kits to amateur constructors.

The fuselage structure of the prototype is basically a surplus Air Force/Navy 200 US gallon drop-tank; but the plans provide for alternative bulkhead/stressed-skin construction for builders unable to obtain a suitable tank. In this form the aircraft is designated DSK-2 Golden Hawk.

The Hawk flew for the first time on 26 May 1973, powered by a 48.5 kW (65 hp) Lycoming engine, but the airframe will accept power plants of up to 93 kW (125 hp). At least 45 Hawks are known to be under construction.

For details: 126 Georgia Place, Fort Walton Beach, Florida 32548, USA.

Four-seat delta-wing sporting monoplane

Data: 134 kW (180 hp) version
Power plant: Prototype has one 134 kW (180 hp) Lycoming O-360 flat-four engine. 149 kW (200 hp) engine optional
Wing span: 6.71 m (22 ft 0 in)
Wing area, gross: 16.07 m² (173 sq ft)
Length overall: 5.79 m (19 ft 0 in)
Width, wings folded: 2.24 m (7 ft 4 in)
Height overall: 1.83 m (6 ft 0 in)
Weight empty, fully equipped: 435 kg (960 lb)
Max T-O weight: 816 kg (1,800 lb)
Max level speed at 2,285 m (7,500 ft): 165 knots (306 km/h; 190 mph)
Max cruising speed at 2,285 m (7,500 ft), with fixed-pitch propeller: 156 knots (290 km/h; 180 mph)
Max rate of climb at S/L: 670 m (2,200 ft)/min
Service ceiling: 4,420 m (14,500 ft)
Range with max fuel and pilot only: 625 nm (1,158 km; 720 miles)
Range with max payload: 390 nm (724 km; 450 miles)
Accommodation: Standard accommodation for pilot, on single forward seat, and three passengers on aft bench seat. Access by upward-opening canopy. Baggage space
Construction: Welded steel tube wing structure, with stainless steel capstrips to which laminated glassfibre skins are secured by Dupont explosive rivets. Aluminium skin and aluminium pop rivets optional. Welded steel tube fuselage structure with stainless steel capstrips and glassfibre skins, except for undersurface which has steel tube capstrips and fabric covering. Welded steel tube tail unit, fabric covered. Retractable landing gear

History: Developed from the delta-wing JD-1, which had been unique among homebuilts, the JD-2 made its first flight in July 1966. Plans for this aircraft are available to amateur constructors, and Mr John Dyke formed Dyke Aircraft to market them. A total of 288 JD-2s were reported to be under construction by early 1976, with examples either under construction or flying in Australia, Brazil, Canada, France, Germany, Japan, New Zealand, South Africa, the UK, and the USA. As further help to the homebuilder, hardware and tubing kits are available

For details: 2840 Old Yellow Springs Road, Fairborn, Ohio 45324, USA.

(USA)

EAA ACRO-SPORT and SUPER ACRO-SPORT

Single-seat aerobatic biplanes

Data: Acro-Sport prototype
Power plant: Prototype has one 134 kW (180 hp) Lycoming engine. Basic power plant is a 74.5 kW (100 hp) Continental O-200 flat-four engine
Wing span: upper   5.97 m (19 ft 7 in)
              lower   5.82 m (19 ft 1 in)
Wing area, gross: 10.73 m² (115.5 sq ft)
Length overall: 5.33 m (17 ft 6 in)
Height overall: 1.83 m (6 ft 0 in)
Weight empty, equipped: 332 kg (733 lb)
Max T-O weight: 612 kg (1,350 lb)
Max level speed: 132 knots (245 km/h; 152 mph)
Max cruising speed: 113 knots (209 km/h; 130 mph)
Max rate of climb at S/L: 1,067 m (3,500 ft)/min
Range with max fuel: 260 nm (482 km; 300 miles)
Accommodation: Single seat in open cockpit. Baggage space behind headrest, 16 kg (35 lb) capacity
Construction: Braced wings of wooden construction, fabric covered. Glassfibre wingtips. Fuselage structure of welded steel tube with wooden stringers, fabric covered. Glassfibre nose cowl and light alloy engine cowling. Braced tail unit of welded steel tube, fabric covered. Non-retractable landing gear

History: The Acro-Sport was designed by Mr Paul Poberezny, President of the EAA, specifically for construction by school students as a pupils' project.

First flight of the prototype Acro-Sport was made on 11 January 1972, only 352 days after its design was started, although it represented a completely new design, unrelated to the EAA Biplane. The prototype demonstrated good flight characteristics, and is a versatile aircraft for sport or aerobatic use. The provision of ailerons on both wings ensures positive aileron response and a high rate of roll.

Plans and construction manuals are available to homebuilders, and more than 400 Acro-Sports are known to be under construction.

The Super Acro-Sport is a developed version, on which work was started in 1971. The first flight was made on 28 March 1973. It is intended for unlimited International Class aerobatic competition at world championship level. Generally similar in appearance to the Acro-Sport, the Super has a more powerful (149 kW; 200 hp) Lycoming IO-360-A2A engine, nearly-symmetrical aerofoil sections, an improved rate of roll and inverted flight capability

For details: PO Box 229, Hales Corners, Wisconsin 53130, USA.

Super Acro-Sport

Single-seat sporting biplane

Data: EAA Biplane Model P. Performance data with 63.5 kW (85 hp) engine

Power plant: Prototype has a 63.5 kW (85 hp) Continental C85-8 flat-four engine. Provision for engines of up to 112 kW (150 hp); but most Model Ps have a 93 kW (125 hp) Lycoming engine

Wing span: 6.10 m (20 ft 0 in)

Wing area, gross: 10.03 m² (108 sq ft)

Length overall: 5.18 m (17 ft 0 in)

Height overall: 1.83 m (6 ft 0 in)

Weight empty: 322 kg (710 lb)

Max T-O weight: 522 kg (1,150 lb)

Max level speed at S/L: 109 knots (201 km/h; 125 mph)

Econ cruising speed: 96 knots (177 km/h; 110 mph)

Max rate of climb at S/L: 305 m (1,000 ft)/min

Service ceiling: 3,500 m (11,500 ft)

Range with max fuel: 304 nm (560 km; 350 miles)

Accommodation: Single seat in open cockpit

Construction: Braced wings of wooden construction, with aluminium leading-edges and fabric covering. Welded steel tube fuselage and tail structures, fabric covered. Non-retractable landing gear

History: The prototype of the EAA Biplane was built between 1957 and May 1960 as a classroom project by students of St Rita's High School, Chicago, under the supervision of Mr Robert Blacker. It flew for the first time on 10 June 1960, powered by a 48.5 kW (65 hp) Continental A65 engine. Due to the fact that the N-shape cabane and I-type interplane struts had not been constructed properly, and that in a change from the original plans a high turtleneck had been added, performance was below expectations. After modifications to the struts, flight testing was resumed on 26 November 1960.

Subsequently, a new metal propeller was fitted, the engine cooling was improved and a cockpit canopy installed. The prototype was then taken over by the EAA, and further changes were made, including installation of a 63.5 kW (85 hp) engine and removal of the cockpit canopy.

Mr Paul Poberezny, President of the EAA, subsequently introduced further modifications which included increasing the area of the tail surfaces. In this form the aircraft is known as the Model P.

Over 7,000 sets of plans of the EAA Biplane have been sold; many examples are flying and under construction throughout the world

For details: PO Box 229, Hales Corners, Wisconsin 53130, USA.

Biplane Model P

Two-seat sporting monoplane

Data: Standard Cougar
Power plant: One 86 kW (115 hp) Lycoming O-235 flat-four engine
Wing span: 6.25 m (20 ft 6 in)
Wing area, gross: 7.66 m² (82.5 sq ft)
Length overall: 5.76 m (18 ft 11 in)
Height overall: 1.68 m (5 ft 6 in)
Weight empty: 283 kg (624 lb)
Max T-O weight: 567 kg (1,250 lb)
Max level speed at S/L: 169 knots (314 km/h; 195 mph)
Max cruising speed at 2,130 m (7,000 ft): 144 knots (267 km/h; 166 mph)
Max rate of climb at S/L: 395 m (1,300 ft)/min
Service ceiling: 3,950 m (13,000 ft)
Range with max fuel: 651 nm (1,207 km; 750 miles)

Accommodation: Two seats side by side in enclosed cabin. Dual controls. Space for 41 kg (90 lb) of baggage
Construction: Braced wooden wings, plywood covered except for fabric covering on trailing-edge. Steel tube fuselage and tail structures, fabric covered. Non-retractable landing gear

History: A prototype side-by-side two-seat light monoplane named the Cougar, designed by Mr Robert Nesmith, flew for the first time in March 1957. Sets of plans were made available to amateur constructors, originally from Mr Nesmith and, since the beginning of 1977, from the EAA. About 250 Cougars were flying or under construction in early 1976. Some incorporate detail modifications. For example, one has a T-tail and others have been completed with folding wings.

For details: PO Box 229, Hales Corners, Wisconsin 53130, USA.

Single-seat sporting monoplane

Power plant: One 44.5 kW (60 hp) Limbach SL 1700 EA flat-four engine
Wing span: 9.09 m (29 ft 10 in)
Wing area, gross: 12.47 m² (134.25 sq ft)
Length overall: 5.26 m (17 ft 3 in)
Height overall: 1.88 m (6 ft 2 in)
Weight empty: 246 kg (543 lb)
Max T-O weight: 408 kg (900 lb)
Max level speed at S/L: 89 knots (166 km/h; 103 mph)
Max cruising speed: 74 knots (137 km/h; 85 mph)
Max rate of climb at S/L: 152 m (500 ft)/min

Range with max fuel: 251 nm (466 km; 290 miles)
Accommodation: Single seat in open cockpit
Construction: Braced parasol wing of wooden construction, fabric covered. Welded steel tube fuselage structure, with wooden formers, fabric covered. Braced tail unit of welded steel tube, fabric covered. Non-retractable landing gear

History: Design and construction of this lightweight sporting aircraft began simultaneously in January 1974, and the first flight was recorded six months later. It is the latest design to emanate from Mr Paul Poberezny, President of the EAA. Plans are available to amateur constructors
For details: PO Box 229, Hales Corners, Wisconsin 53130, USA.

P-9 Pixie with 1,500 cc Volkswagen engine

Single-seat and two-seat light monoplanes

Data: VP-1. Performance figures for VP-1 powered by a 30 kW (40 hp) engine, at 295 kg (650 lb) T-O weight
Power plant: One 30, 39.5 or 44.5 kW (40, 53 or 60 hp) modified Volkswagen motor car engine
Wing span: 7.32 m (24 ft 0 in)
Wing area, gross: 9.29 m² (100 sq ft)
Length overall: 5.49 m (18 ft 0 in)
Height overall: 1.56 m (5 ft 1½ in)
Weight empty: 200 kg (440 lb)
Max T-O weight: 340 kg (750 lb)
Cruising speed: 65 knots (121 km/h; 75 mph)
Max rate of climb at S/L: 122 m (400 ft)/min
Accommodation: Single seat in open cockpit
Construction: Strut-braced wooden wings, fabric covered. All-wood fuselage. Glassfibre fairing aft of pilot's seat. Tail unit of basically wooden construction, fabric covered. Non-retractable landing gear

History: Mr W.S. Evans designed the VP-1 with the idea of producing for the novice homebuilder an all-wood aircraft that would be easy to build and safe to fly. He was prepared to sacrifice both appearance and performance to achieve this aim. Two years of spare-time design and a year of construction produced the prototype VP-1 monoplane.
This was powered originally by a 30 kW (40 hp) Volkswagen engine, but was subsequently re-engined with a 39.5 kW (53 hp) Volkswagen, giving an improved rate of climb of 183 m (600 ft)/min at sea level.
Mr Evans next developed a two-seat version of the design, known as the VP-2. This is generally similar to the single-seat model, but is powered by a 44.5/48.5 kW (60/65 hp) Volkswagen engine. In other respects the VP-2 has only minor variations from the VP-1, although it is a larger aircraft in terms of dimensions and weights.
Plans for both models are available to amateur constructors

For details: PO Box 744, La Jolla, California 92038, USA.

VP-1

Single-seat or two-seat sporting monoplane

Power plant: One 63.5 kW (85 hp) Continental C85-8 flat-four engine
Wing span: 6.82 m (22 ft 4½ in)
Wing area, gross: 13.29 m² (143.10 sq ft)
Length overall: 5.84 m (19 ft 2 in)
Height overall: 1.73 m (5 ft 8 in)
Weight empty: 313 kg (690 lb)
Normal T-O weight: 499 kg (1,100 lb)
Max level speed at S/L: 104 knots (193 km/h; 120 mph)
Cruising speed: 83 knots (153 km/h; 95 mph)
Max rate of climb at S/L: 305 m (1,000 ft)/min
Service ceiling: over 3,050 m (10,000 ft)
Range with max fuel, 15 min reserve: 390 nm (724 km; 450 miles)
Accommodation: Pilot (with provision for passenger seated in tandem) in enclosed cabin. Baggage compartment aft of cabin. Overhead control assembly permits sleeping in the cabin after removing or collapsing seat
Construction: All-wood geodetic wing structure, fabric covered. Welded steel tube fuselage and tail unit structures, fabric covered. Standard Piper J-3 non-retractable landing gear

History: Mr W.J. Fike has designed and built five light aircraft since 1929. In 1953 he began the design of an aircraft to evaluate the flight characteristics of a low aspect ratio (3.0) wing of only 9% thickness/chord ratio when applied to a low-power monoplane of high-wing configuration. The wing, of wooden geodetic construction, is so designed that various wingtips may be installed for evaluation. A standard Piper J-3 tail unit is utilised; but this is modified to keep the tailplane span within the 2.44 m (8 ft) limit allowed by US highway regulations for towed vehicles. A secondary objective of the Model "E" project was to develop a low-cost easy-to-build two-seat lightplane. The wing can be removed within ten minutes to enable the aircraft to be towed by a motor vehicle or for storage in an ordinary garage.

Construction of the Model "E" extended over a period of seven years and it was completed in early 1970, the first flight taking place on 22 March 1970. After a time Mr Fike re-engined the aircraft with a 63.5 kW (85 hp) Continental C85-8 engine, and it made its first flight with this power plant on 6 June 1971. It had accumulated a total of 188 flight hours by early 1975, but other work commitments prevented more than 7½ hours of flight testing throughout that year.

During 1974 Mr Fike added 0.36 m (1 ft 2 in) wingtip extensions and, at a later stage of flight testing, flat endplates were added to the wingtips. The extensions to the wing have been shown to enhance performance, but the effect of the endplates proved negligible. Plans for the Model "E" are available to amateur constructors

For details: PO Box 683, Anchorage, Alaska 99510, USA.

Ultra-light sporting monoplane

Power plant: One 30 kW (40 hp) Volkswagen 1,500 cc flat-four engine
Wing span: 8.64 m (28 ft 0 in)
Wing area, gross: 10.68 m² (115 sq ft)
Length overall: 4.78 m (15 ft 8 in)
Height overall: 2.13 m (7 ft 0 in)
Weight empty: 177 kg (390 lb)
Max T-O weight: 295 kg (650 lb)
Max level speed: 78 knots (145 km/h; 90 mph)
Max cruising speed: 69 knots (129 km/h; 80 mph)
Max rate of climb at S/L: 183 m (600 ft)/min
Range with max fuel: 152 nm (282 km; 175 miles)
Accommodation: Single seat in cockpit protected by deep windscreen
Construction: Wooden wing structure with aluminium leading-edge, plywood covered. Wooden fuselage structure, with plywood covering in the forward cockpit area and fabric covering aft. All-wood tail unit. Non-retractable landing gear

History: Design of the Scooter began in July 1965, and construction was started in November of the same year. The prototype was powered originally by a 13.5 kW (18 hp) Cushman golf-kart engine, and it was with this power plant that the first flight was made in June 1967. Performance was marginal, so Mr K. Flaglor replaced the Cushman with a 27 kW (36 hp) Volkswagen engine. The current power plant develops 30 kW (40 hp). When flown to the 1967 EAA meet at Rockford, Illinois, the Scooter won the 'Outstanding Ultra-Light' and 'Outstanding Volkswagen-Powered Airplane' awards. Plans are available to amateur constructors from Ace Aircraft Manufacturing Company

For details: 106 Arthur Road, Asheville, North Carolina 28806, USA.

Scooter with 1,600 cc Volkswagen engine

Two-seat lightweight amphibian

Data: Stage III aircraft
Power plant: One 67 kW (90 hp) Continental C90 flat-four engine.
Provision for engines of 63.5-93 kW (85-125 hp)
Wing span: 11.89 m (39 ft 0 in)
Wing area, gross: 18.1 m² (195 sq ft)
Length overall: 7.62 m (25 ft 0 in)
Height overall: 2.68 m (8 ft 9½ in)
Weight empty: 544 kg (1,200 lb)
Max T-O weight: 771 kg (1,700 lb)
Max level speed at S/L: 82 knots (153 km/h; 95 mph)
Max cruising speed: 74 knots (137 km/h; 85 mph)
Max rate of climb at S/L: 152 m (500 ft)/min
Service ceiling: 3,660 m (12,000 ft)
Range with max fuel: 260 nm (482 km; 300 miles)
Accommodation: Two seats side by side in enclosed cockpit
Construction: Braced wing structure; light alloy main spar and aerofoil of solid sculptured styrofoam, with glassfibre covering overall. Light alloy fuselage structure, stiffened with styrofoam and covered with glassfibre. Specially designed floats, one each side of fuselage undersurface, are integral with fuselage structure. Retractable landing gear

History: Flight Dynamics Inc designed and developed this unusual amphibian, of which plans are available to amateur constructors. It can be built in Stage I unpowered configuration with a flexible wing, in which form it is towed into the air by a motor boat. In Stage II configuration a power plant is added, enabling the aircraft to be flown from land or water. The final Stage III configuration substitutes a conventional fixed wing in place of the flexible wing.
Flight Dynamics claims that the simplified method of Stage I construction enables the homebuilder to get the aircraft into the air in a minimum of time, and that it can be completed in more sophisticated form as time and finances allow. Design began in January 1966; construction of the prototype started in March 1967, and the first flight was made in October 1970

For details: PO Box 5070, State Collage Station, Raleigh, North Carolina 27607, USA.

Two/three-seat light monoplane

Power plant: One 157 kW (210 hp) Continental IO-360-A flat-six engine
Wing span: 7.04 m (23 ft 1 in)
Wing area, gross: 8.55 m² (92 sq ft)
Length overall: 6.50 m (21 ft 4 in)
Height overall: 2.57 m (8 ft 5 in)
Weight empty, equipped: 621 kg (1,370 lb)
Max T-O weight: 1,270 kg (2,800 lb)
Max level speed at S/L: 183 knots (340 km/h; 211 mph)
Max cruising speed at 1,980 m (6,500 ft): 176 knots (327 km/h; 203 mph)
Max rate of climb at S/L: 549 m (1,800 ft)/min
Service ceiling: 6,400 m (21,000 ft)
Range with max fuel, no reserve: 2,952 nm (5,470 km; 3,400 miles)
Accommodation: Two seats side by side beneath transparent canopy. Space for 91 kg (200 lb) of baggage aft of seats, or for a third passenger on a removable jump-seat. Cabin is heated and ventilated

Construction: All-metal construction. Glassfibre nose cowl and fairings. Retractable landing gear

History: Mr Peter Garrison was a contributor to the initial design of the Practavia Sprite when employed in London. After his return to the USA he modified and developed this basic design, and the first flight of the resulting Melmoth was made on 6 September 1973.
Comparison of the two designs reveals to a small degree their common parentage; but whereas the Sprite is a simply-constructed lightplane for amateur builders, the Melmoth could be described more accurately as a lightplane research prototype. It includes such aerodynamic features as double-slotted Fowler trailing-edge flaps and adjustable-incidence ailerons. Special systems and equipment include automatic fuel balancing, remote compass, Century I autopilot, full IFR panel and extensive communication radios.
A second, four-seat, example of Melmoth is being built in Texas by an acquaintance of Mr Garrison. It is not the intention, however, to make plans available to amateur constructors

For details of Practavia Sprite: Wycombe Air Park, Booker, near Marlow, Buckinghamshire, England.

(France)

GATARD STATOPLAN AG 02 POUSSIN (CHICK)

Single-seat ultra-light monoplane

Power plant: One 18 kW (24 hp) modified Volkswagen flat-four engine
Wing span: 6.40 m (21 ft 0 in)
Wing area, gross: 6.15 m² (66.2 sq ft)
Length overall: 4.53 m (14 ft 10½ in)
Height overall: 1.50 m (4 ft 11 in)
Weight empty: 170 kg (375 lb)
Max T-O weight: 280 kg (617 lb)
Max cruising speed: 77 knots (144 km/h; 89 mph)
Max speed for aerobatics: 69 knots (130 km/h; 80 mph)
Max rate of climb at S/L: 132 m (435 ft)/min
Accommodation: Single seat under large rearward-sliding transparent canopy. Baggage space aft of seat
Construction: Wooden structure, plywood covered. Non-retractable landing gear

History: M Albert Gatard built two prototypes of the Poussin; the information above applies to the second of these, which introduced a number of design improvements. Flight tests revealed excellent aerobatic qualities and the power plant has been modified to permit up to 20 seconds of inverted flying.

This prototype of the Poussin was extensively flight-tested at the Centre d'Essais en Vol at Istres, and the performance figures quoted are those which were obtained during these tests. As a result of recommendations by the CEV, a 27 kW (36 hp) Rectimo (modified Volkswagen VW 1,200) engine is suggested as the most suitable power plant for use by amateur constructors of the Poussin. The second prototype has been re-engined with a 1,200 cc VW, and this installation is expected to improve the CG position as well as making possible a max speed of approx 92 knots (170 km/h; 106 mph) and a rate of climb of 210 m (690 ft)/min.

Several Poussins are being built by amateur constructors, and three were known to be nearing completion in 1975. One of them is the work of Mr Gomès of Lubumbashi in the Zaïre Republic.

Like all of M Gatard's designs, the Poussin has a unique control system which involves the use of a variable-incidence lifting tailplane of large area. Instead of altering the wing angle of attack to increase lift, the pilot lowers full-span slotted aileron/flaps and adjusts the tailplane to maintain pitching equilibrium. In consequence, the aircraft climbs with the fuselage datum at no more than 4° to horizontal, which preserves a good forward view and low body drag

For details: 52 route de Jonzac, 17130-Montendre, France

Two-seat sporting monoplane

Power plant: One 93 kW (125 hp) Lycoming O-290-G flat-four engine
Wing span: 10.97m (36 ft 0 in)
Length overall: 7.32 m (24 ft 0 in)
Weight empty: 447 kg (985 lb)
Max T-O weight: 671 kg (1,480 lb)
Cruising speed: 61 knots (113 km/h; 70 mph)
Max rate of climb at S/L: 122 m (400 ft)/min
Accommodation: Two seats in tandem in open cockpits
Construction: Braced parasol wing, fabric covered. Welded steel tube fuselage and tail structures, fabric covered. Non-retractable landing gear

History: Richard Halpin and Tom Huf, of Hatboro and Ivyland, Pennsylvania respectively, designed and built the H and H Special which they describe as a 'fun' aircraft.

The engine, which is mounted on struts aft of the wing, drives a two-blade fixed-pitch pusher propeller, and the cylindrical fuel tank is strut-mounted above the wing centre-section. The wing itself is supported by multiple centre-section struts. Little further information is available on this aircraft that cannot be deduced from the accompanying illustration, although it is known that the Special takes off after a run of only 91 m (300 ft) and lands in 61 m (200 ft)

Single-seat sporting monoplane

Power plant: One 44.5 kW (60 hp) Franklin 4AC-171 flat-four engine
Wing span: 8.08 m (26 ft 6 in)
Length overall: 5.33 m (17 ft 6 in)
Height overall: 2.03 m (6 ft 8 in)
Weight empty: 272 kg (600 lb)
Max T-O weight: 399 kg (880 lb)
Max level speed: 91 knots (169 km/h; 105 mph)
Cruising speed: 74 knots (137 km/h; 85 mph)
Max rate of climb at S/L: 183 m (600 ft)/min

Range: 195 nm (362 km; 225 miles)
Accommodation: Single seat in open cockpit
Construction: Braced parasol wing of wooden construction, Dacron covered. Conventional wooden fuselage structure, Dacron covered. Braced tail unit of welded steel tube construction, Dacron covered. Non-retractable landing gear

History: Mr George Hast designed and built this sporting monoplane, which he named the Wooden Baby. Of original design, it incorporates features of several parasol-wing homebuilts, and was constructed over a period of 10 years at a cost of approximately $1,500.

Two-seat lightweight biplane

Power plant: One 112 kW (150 hp) Lycoming O-320 flat-four engine
Wing span, both: 7.92 m (26 ft 0 in)
Wing area, gross: 17.65 m² (190 sq ft)
Length overall: 5.64 m (18 ft 6 in)
Height overall: 2.39 m (7 ft 10 in)
Weight empty: 438 kg (966 lb)
Max T-O weight: 726 kg (1,600 lb)
Max cruising speed: 87 knots (161 km/h; 100 mph)
Max rate of climb at S/L: 366 m (1,200 ft)/min
Range with max fuel, 30 min reserve: 234 nm (434 km; 270 miles)
Accommodation: Two seats in tandem in open cockpits

Construction: Braced wooden wings, fabric covered. Welded steel tube fuselage and tail unit, fabric covered. Non-retractable landing gear

History: Design and construction of this biplane, by Mr John D. Hatz, started in September 1959, and FAA certification in the Experimental (amateur-built) category was awarded on 18 April 1968. First flight of the CB-1 was made on the following day, powered by a 63.5 kW (85 hp) Continental C85-12 engine; this has since been replaced with a Lycoming O-320 engine.
Plans are available to amateur constructors and many CB-1s are being built

For details: Merrill Airways, Municipal Airport, Merrill, Wisconsin 54452, USA.

Single-seat ultra-light biplane

Power plant: One 10.5 kW (14 hp) McCulloch 101A single-cylinder engine
Wing span, both: 5.18 m (17 ft 0 in)
Wing area, gross: 9.10 m² (98 sq ft)
Length overall: 4.27 m (14 ft 0 in)
Height overall: 1.68 m (5 ft 6 in)
Weight empty, inc fuel: 55.5 kg (123 lb)
Max T-O weight: 140 kg (310 lb)
Max level speed at S/L: 43.5 knots (80.5 km/h; 50 mph)
Econ cruising speed at S/L: 35 knots (64.5 km/h; 40 mph)
Service ceiling: 1,220 m (4,000 ft)
Range: 17 nm (32 km; 20 miles)
Accommodation: Single seat in open position
Construction: Braced composite wing structure of wooden spars, light alloy tubular ribs, a leading-edge faired in with rigid urethane foam and fabric covering. Wooden closed box-structure fuselage, with aluminium tube tailboom, filled with urethane foam. Braced tail unit. Tailplane consists of a single piece of Foam Core sheet, made of styrofoam core sandwiched between high-strength craft paper. Fin and rudder of similar construction. Stressed areas of tail unit reinforced by plywood sheet. Non-retractable landing gear

History: Mr R.W. Hovey's objective when designing the Whing Ding was to produce an aircraft which would require minimal construction time, would offer STOL performance, and would be capable of rapid disassembly for transportation. To achieve these ends the design has some unusual features, such as wing warping for roll control, use of an aluminium tube tailboom made of high-strength light alloy sheet and urethane foam stiffening, and the use of styrofoam core sandwiched in craft paper for the tail surfaces.
Design began in October 1970, with construction starting in the following month. First flight was made in February 1971, at which time the aircraft received FAA certification in the Experimental category.
The original prototype was sold in Japan, where considerable interest has been aroused among homebuilders. A second prototype was completed subsequently. More than 4,000 sets of plans have been sold, and at least 300 Whing Dings were under construction by February 1976

For details: PO Box 1074, Saugus, California 91350, USA.

Single-seat light biplane

Data: Prototype
Power plant: One 93 kW (125 hp) Lycoming O-290 flat-four engine
Wing span: upper   6.40 m (21 ft 0 in)
           lower   5.54 m (18 ft 2 in)
Wing area: 11.50 m² (123.8 sq ft)
Length overall: 5.87 m (19 ft 3 in)
Height over tail (flying attitude): 2.16 m (7 ft 1 in)
Weight empty: 322 kg (710 lb)
Max permissible T-O weight: 450 kg (1,000 lb)
Max level speed: 100 knots (185 km/h; 115 mph)
Max rate of climb at S/L: 488 m (1,600 ft)/min
Accommodation: Single seat in open cockpit. Space for light baggage aft of seat
Construction: Wooden structure, fabric covered except for fuselage which is plywood covered. Non-retractable landing gear

History: Design of the Isaacs Fury was started in January 1961, as a 7/10th scale wooden biplane replica of the Hawker Fury biplane fighter of the 1930s; construction of the aircraft began in April of the same year. It flew for the first time on 30 August 1963, powered by a 48.5 kW (65 hp) Walter Mikron engine. In 1966-67 Mr Isaacs modified the Fury prototype to Mk II standard, by re-stressing the airframe and installing the present Lycoming engine; the aircraft flew in this form in the Summer of 1967. It was subsequently acquired by Mr W. Raper of Wrotham, Kent, who made further refinements, including the addition of blister fairings over the engine cylinders. It is now owned by Mr D. Toms, and is based at Land's End airfield. Constructional drawings for the Fury II are available to amateur builders. Several other Furies have flown and more are under construction in the UK. Three are known to be under construction or flying in New Zealand; one in Jersey; and others in the USA and Canada

For details: 42 Landguard Road, Southampton, Hampshire SO1 5DP, England.

Single-seat sporting monoplane

Power plant: One 74.5 kW (100 hp) Continental O-200 flat-four engine, or alternative engine in same category
Wing span: 6.75 m (22 ft 1½ in)
Wing area, gross: 8.08 m² (87 sq ft)
Length overall: 5.88 m (19 ft 3 in)
Height overall: 1.73 m (5 ft 8 in)
Weight empty: 366 kg (805 lb)
Max T-O weight: 499 kg (1,100 lb)
Max level speed: 130 knots (240 km/h; 150 mph)
Cruising speed: 116 knots (215 km/h; 134 mph)

Max rate of climb at S/L: 336 m (1,100 ft)/min
Accommodation: Single seat under blister-type transparent canopy. Space for light baggage aft of seat
Construction: Wooden structure, plywood covered. Non-retractable landing gear on prototype

History: Construction of the prototype ⁶/₁₀-scale Spitfire began in the Summer of 1969, and it flew for the first time on 5 May 1975. The airframe is stressed to meet the aerobatic requirements of $+9g$ and $-4.5g$ (factored) as laid down in BCAR

For details: 42 Landguard Road, Southampton, Hampshire SO1 5DP, England.

(USA)

Single-seat sporting monoplane

Power plant: One 48.5 kW (65 hp) Continental A65 flat-four engine
Wing span: 5.69 m (18 ft 8 in)
Length overall: 4.90 m (16 ft 1 in)
Height overall: 2.06 m (6 ft 9 in)
Weight empty: 236 kg (520 lb)
Max T-O weight: 372 kg (820 lb)
Max level speed: 109 knots (201 km/h; 125 mph)
Cruising speed: 100 knots (185 km/h; 115 mph)
Max rate of climb at S/L: 274 m (900 ft)/min
Endurance: 4 hours

JAMESON RJJ-1 GYPSY HAWK

Accommodation: Single seat under transparent cockpit canopy
Construction: All-metal construction. Non-retractable landing gear

History: Mr Richard J. Jameson designed this aircraft, of which he intends to make plans available to amateur constructors. Design emphasis has been on simplicity of construction, light alloy angle being used to fabricate the wing spar, as well as the basic structures of the fuselage and tail unit. The Gypsy Hawk prototype took three and a half years to build and cost under $2,000.

For details: 124-C North Stanford Avenue, Fullerton, California 92631, USA.

(Poland)

JANOWSKI J-1 DON KICHOT and J-2 POLONEZ

Single-seat ultra-light monoplanes

Data: J-1 Don Kichot
Power plant: One 17 kW (23 hp) Janowski Saturn 500B two-cylinder two-stroke engine
Wing span: 7.60 m (24 ft 11¼ in)
Wing area, gross: 7.50 m² (80.7 sq ft)
Length overall: 4.88 m (16 ft 0 in)
Height overall: 1.40 m (4 ft 7 in)
Weight empty: 163 kg (359 lb)
Max T-O weight: 270 kg (595 lb)
Max level speed at S/L: 73 knots (135 km/h; 84 mph)
Max cruising speed: 65 knots (120 km/h; 75 mph)
Max rate of climb at S/L: 120 m (390 ft)/min
Service ceiling: 2,500 m (8,200 ft)
Range: 134 nm (250 km; 155 miles)

G **limits:** +4.0; −1.5
Accommodation: Single seat in enclosed cockpit
Construction: Wooden structure, covered with fabric and wood. Non-retractable landing gear

History: Mr Jaroslaw Janowski, assisted by Mr Witold Kalita, designed and built a light amateur-built aircraft known as the J-1 Don Kichot (Don Quixote). Work on the project was started in 1967, and the aircraft flew for the first time on 30 July 1970. Two additional J-1s are reportedly being built by amateur constructors: one by Mr Michal Offierski, a pre-war Polish holder of international powered sailplane records, and one by Mr T. Wood in the UK.
In 1971 Mr Janowski designed a second single-seat aircraft known as the J-2 Polonez. This is smaller than the J-1, but is of generally similar configuration except for its mid-mounted wings and T-tail. A prototype is under construction.

J-1 Don Kichot

Two/three-seat sporting biplane

Data: Prototype with 134 kW (180 hp) Lycoming engine
Power plant: Prototype has one 134 kW (180 hp) Lycoming O-360 flat-four engine. Provision for alternative engines up to 157 kW (210 hp)
Wing span, upper: 7.32 m (24 ft 0 in)
Wing area, gross: 17.2 m² (185 sq ft)
Length overall: 5.87 m (19 ft 3 in)
Height overall: 2.18 m (7 ft 2 in)
Weight empty: 580 kg (1,280 lb)
Max T-O weight: 907 kg (2,000 lb)
Max level speed at S/L: 122 knots (225 km/h; 140 mph)
Max cruising speed: 110 knots (204 km/h; 127 mph)
Max rate of climb at S/L: 518 m (1,700 ft)/min
Accommodation: Two seats side by side in open cockpit. Provision for tandem two-seat or three-seat configurations. Drawings available for rearward-sliding transparent cockpit canopy. Dual controls standard. Baggage compartment aft of seats with 54 kg (120 lb) capacity. Baggage locker in turtleback, capacity 9 kg (20 lb)
Construction: Braced wings of composite wood and light alloy construction, fabric covered. Welded steel tube fuselage (with light alloy stringers) and tail structures, fabric covered. Non-retractable landing gear

History: Following equipment manufacture, aircraft development work and the restoration of a Curtiss Robin aircraft, the Javelin Aircraft Company began the development of a biplane of its own design on 1 January 1964. The resulting aircraft, named Wichawk, has structural geometry similar to that of a Stearman biplane, as well as some of the latter's aerodynamic features, and is stressed for +12 and −6g. It flew for the first time on 24 May 1971 and has received FAA certification in the Experimental (homebuilt) category. Javelin Aircraft does not build the Wichawk, but plans, wing ribs and fuel tanks are available to amateur constructors. More than 100 Wichawks are known to be under construction

For details: 9175 East Douglas, Wichita, Kansas 67207, USA

Two-seat sporting monoplane

Power plant: One 164 kW (220 hp) Lycoming GO-435-2 flat-four engine
Wing span: 7.54 m (24 ft 9 in)
Wing area, gross: 11.15 m² (120 sq ft)
Length overall: 6.55 m (21 ft 6 in)
Weight empty: 678 kg (1,495 lb)
Max T-O weight: 998 kg (2,200 lb)
Max level speed at 2,135 m (7,000 ft): 189 knots (351 km/h; 218 mph)
Max cruising speed at 2,135 m (7,000 ft): 174 knots (322 km/h; 200 mph)
Max rate of climb at S/L: 670 m (2,200 ft)/min

Accommodation: Two seats side by side under upward-hinged canopy. Baggage space behind seats. Cabin heated and ventilated
Construction: Wing structure of wood and ply. Ailerons of wood and glassfibre construction. Wooden fuselage structure with ply skin. Wooden tail unit with glassfibre tips. Retractable landing gear

History: Design of this light aircraft began in August 1966, and construction of the prototype commenced in June 1969. The first flight of the Barracuda was made on 29 June 1975, and it is certificated in the Experimental category. Plans are available to amateur constructors, and by February 1976 several more Barracudas were being built.
For details: PO Box 975, Renton, Washington 98055, USA.

Single-seat light monoplanes

Power plant: One 18.5 kW (25 hp) Poinsard (D.9) or modified Volkswagen (D.92) flat-four engine; other engines of 18.5-48.5 kW (25-65 hp) can be fitted, including the 27 kW (36 hp) Aeronca JAP and Continental A40
Wing span: 7.00 m (22 ft 11 in)
Wing area, gross: 9.0 m² (96.8 sq ft)
Length overall: 5.45 m (17 ft 10½ in)
Weight empty: 190 kg (420 lb)
Max T-O weight: 320 kg (705 lb)
Max level speed at S/L (30 kW; 40 hp engine): 87 knots (160 km/n; 100 mph)
Cruising speed (30 kW; 40 hp engine): 74 knots (137 km/h; 85 mph)
Max rate of climb at S/L (30 kW; 40 hp engine): 180 m (590 ft)/min
Range with max fuel (30 kW; 40 hp engine): 217 nm (400 km; 250 miles)
Accommodation: Single seat in open cockpit
Construction: Wooden wing structure, fabric covered. Wooden fuselage. Wooden tail unit, plywood and fabric covered. Non-retractable landing gear

History: Following formation of the Société des Avions Jodel in March 1946, the company designed and built the D.9 Bébé light monoplane, which made its first flight in January 1948. This aeroplane, which is certificated with various power plants, is intended for amateur construction and can be built in as little as 500 man-hours. The type designation of the Bébé varies according to the type of engine fitted. The original version, with the 18.5 kW (25 hp) Poinsard engine, was designated D.9; the D.92 has a modified Volkswagen engine

For details: 36, Route de Seurre, 21- Beaune, France.

D.9 version

Two-seat monoplanes

Data: Jodel D.11 built by Wayne Nelson of Bountiful, Utah

Power plant: One · 48.5 kW (65 hp) Continental A65-8 flat-four engine

Wing span: 8.23 m (27 ft 0 in)

Weight empty: 340 kg (750 lb)

Max T-O weight: 562 kg (1,240 lb)

Max level speed at S/L: 93 knots (173 km/h; 108 mph)

Cruising speed: 86 knots (161 km/h; 100 mph)

Max rate of climb at S/L: 152 m (500 ft)/min

Service ceiling: 4,875 m (16,000 ft)

Range with max fuel: 260 nm (482 km; 300 miles)

Accommodation: Two seats side by side in enclosed cabin

Construction: Wooden structure; wings covered with Dacron, fuselage and tail unit covered with glassfibre. Non-retractable landing gear

History: As a result of official tests with a Jodel D.9, the French authorities placed an order for the development and construction of two prototypes of a two-seat model – the D.11 fitted with a 33.5 kW (45 hp) Salmson, and the D.111 with a 56 kW (75 hp) Minié engine. The D.11 became the basic model in the series of Jodel two-seaters for amateur and commercial production. A version for amateur construction with a 67 kW (90 hp) Continental engine is the D.119. The D.11 built by Wayne Nelson cost $2,000. Basic structure is of wood, with Dacron covering on the wings and glassfibre covering on the fuselage and tail unit. Changes from the standard D.11 design include the addition of a fixed tail fin forward of the rudder, and of cantilever spring main landing gear legs

For details: 36, Route de Seurre, 21-Beaune, France.

D.11 version

(France)

JURCA M.J.2 and M.J.20 TEMPÊTE

Single-seat light monoplane

Data: Performance figures with 48.5 kW (65 hp) engine
Power plant: One 48.5 kW (65 hp) Continental A65 flat-four engine. Provision for fitting 56, 63.5, 67, or 74.5 kW (75, 85, 90, or 100 hp) Continental, 78.5 or 86 kW (105 or 115 hp) Potez or 93 kW (125 hp) Lycoming engine
Wing span: 6.00 m (19 ft 8 in)
Wing area, gross: 7.98 m^2 (85.90 sq ft)
Length overall: 5.855 m (19 ft 2½ in)
Height over tail: 2.40 m (7 ft 10 in)
Weight empty: 290 kg (639 lb)
Max T-O weight: 430 kg (950 lb)
Max level speed: 104 knots (193 km/h; 120 mph)
Cruising speed: 89 knots (165 km/h; 102 mph)
Max rate of climb at S/L: 170 m (555 ft)/min
Service ceiling: 3,500 m (11,500 ft)
Endurance: 3 hr 20 min
Accommodation: Single seat under long rearward-sliding transparent canopy
Construction: Wooden wing structure, fabric covered. Wooden fuselage structure, plywood covered. Wooden tail structure, plywood and fabric covered. Non-retractable landing gear

History: The prototype Tempête was flown for the first time by its designer, M Marcel Jurca, on 27 June 1956. It obtained its certificate of airworthiness very quickly, and a total of at least 28

Tempêtes are flying, with 20 more under construction, in France, Denmark, Luxembourg, Portugal, the UK, the United States, and Canada, all amateur-built.
The type of engine fitted to a particular aircraft is indicated by a suffix letter in its designation. Suffix letters are A for the 48.5 kW (65 hp) Continental A65, B for the 56 kW (75 hp) Continental A75, C for the 63.5 kW (85 hp) Continental C85, D for the 67 kW (90 hp) Continental C90-14F, E for the 74.5 kW (100 hp) Continental O-200-A, F for the 78.5 kW (105 hp) Potez 4 E-20, G for the 86 kW (115 hp) Potez 4 E-30, and H for the 93 kW (125 hp) Lycoming.
The standard version is the M.J.2A. The M.J.2D can perform aerobatics without loss of height. The Tempête built in Portugal is an M.J.2D; that under construction in Denmark is designated M.J.20, and has a 134 kW (180 hp) engine and a strengthened airframe.
The Tempête is basically a single-seat aircraft but the 112 and 134 kW (150 and 180 hp) versions have provision for carrying on cross-country flights a second person weighing not more than 70 kg (154 lb). They are intended to have an aerobatic capability adequate to compete with American Pitts Specials in international competitions

For details: 2, rue des Champs Philippe, 92-La Garenne-Colombes (Seine), France.
North America: 581 Helen Street, Mt Morris, Michigan 48458 USA.
Australia/New Zealand: Mr Steve Rankin, RD9, Whangarei, New Zealand.

M.J.2 Tempête

Two-seat light monoplane

Data: Modified Sirocco with 86 kW (115 hp) Lycoming O-235-C2B engine built by Luftsportgruppe Liebherr-Aero-Technik (LAT) of Germany

Power plant: One 86 kW (115 hp) Lycoming O-235-C2B engine. Provision for fitting 67 or 74.5 kW (90 or 100 hp) Continental, 78.5 or 86 kW (105 or 115 hp) Potez, 78.5 kW (105 hp) Hirth, 93, 119 or 134 kW (125, 160, or 180 hp) Lycoming, 101 kW (135 hp) Regnier, or 164 kW (220 hp) Franklin engine

Wing span: 7.00 m (23 ft 0 in)
Wing area, gross: 10.00 m² (107.64 sq ft)
Length overall: 6.15 m (20 ft 2 in)
Height overall, tail up: 2.60 m (8 ft 6¼ in)
Weight empty: 430 kg (947 lb)
Max T-O weight: 680 kg (1,499 lb)
Max level speed: 127 knots (235 km/h; 146 mph)
Cruising speed: 116 knots (215 km/h; 134 mph)
Climb to 1,000 m (3,280 ft): 4 min
Service ceiling: 5,000 m (16,400 ft)
Endurance: 4 hr 20 min
Accommodation: Two seats in tandem
Construction: Similar to Tempête. Optional retractable landing gear

History: The M.J.5 Sirocco was developed from the Tempête as a potential club training and touring aircraft. It is fully aerobatic when flown as a two-seater.

The prototype flew for the first time on 3 August 1962, powered by a 78.5 kW (105 hp) Potez 4 E-20 engine. However, it was re-engined with a 119 kW (160 hp) Lycoming O-320 engine and given a retractable landing gear in 1966. Again, it was subsequently re-engined with a 134 kW (180 hp) Lycoming. By mid-February 1967, five more Siroccos were flying, one of them factory-built at Nancy. As the Sirocco was regarded as a basic trainer suitable for amateur construction, official tests were completed and the aircraft was awarded a certificate of airworthiness in the Utility category. A full C of A, covering aerobatic requirements and unlimited spinning, is applicable only when a power plant of 86 kW (115 hp) minimum rating is installed.

At least 40 Siroccos are reported to be flying or under construction by amateurs in France, Canada, Germany, Switzerland, the UK and the United States, with various engines

For details: 2, rue des Champs Philippe, 92-La Garenne-Colombes (Seine), France.

M.J.5 H2 Sirocco

(USA)

Single-seat sporting monoplane

Data: Lark-1B with a 48.5 kW (65 hp) Continental engine
Power plant: Provision for alternative flat-four engines of 48.5-74.5 kW (65-100 hp). Lark-1Bs are flying with Continental A65 (as above), the 56 kW (75 hp) A75-8 and 74.5 kW (100 hp) O-200 engines
Wing span: 7.01 m (23 ft 0 in)
Wing area, gross: 7.48 m² (80.5 sq ft)
Length overall: 5.18 m (17 ft 0 in)
Height overall: 1.65 m (5 ft 5 in)
Weight empty: 249 kg (550 lb)
Max T-O weight: 387 kg (855 lb)
Max level speed: 115 knots (212 km/h; 132 mph)
Max cruising speed: 103 knots (192 km/h; 119 mph)
Max rate of climb at S/L: 274 m (900 ft)/min
Service ceiling: 5,950 m (19,500 ft)
Range with max payload, with reserve: 303 nm (563 km; 350 miles)

Accommodation: Single seat in enclosed cockpit under sliding canopy. Lowered turtledeck and bubble canopy optional. Space for 9 kg (20 lb) of baggage aft of seat
Construction: Braced wing of wooden construction, fabric covered. Welded steel tube fuselage and tail unit structures, fabric covered (stressed to over 6 *g*). Non-retractable landing gear

History: In the early 1960s Mr J. Keleher designed and built a sporting monoplane which he called the Lark. The design was revised in 1963, and the current model, for which plans are available to amateur constructors, is designated Lark-1B.

The Lark-1B built by Mr Parker Warren of Pompano Beach, Florida, is powered by a 74.5 kW (100 hp) Continental O-200 engine and, as such, is worth noting for its comparative performance. Construction was spread over five years and cost approximately $4,000. It differs from the standard aircraft by having a modified tail planform. With a maximum take-off weight of 476 kg (1,050 lb), this Lark-1B has a maximum level speed of 130 knots (241 km/h; 150 mph) and a rate of climb at S/L of 305 m (1,000 ft)/min

For details: 4321 Ogden Drive, Fremont, California 94538, USA.

Two-seat light monoplane

Power plant: Prototype has one 74.5 kW (100 hp) 1.600 cc Volkswagen modified motor car engine
Wing span: 8.08 m (26 ft 6 in)
Wing area, gross: 10.59 m² (114 sq ft)
Length overall: 5.94 m (19 ft 6 in)
Height overall: 1.89 m (6 ft 2½ in)
Weight empty: 358 kg (790 lb)
Max T-O weight: 565 kg (1,246 lb)
Max level speed: 100 knots (185 km/h; 115 mph)
Max cruising speed: 91 knots (169 km/h; 105 mph)
Max rate of climb at S/L: 168 m (550 ft)/min
Service ceiling (estimated): 3.660 m (12.000 ft)
Range: 456 nm (845 km; 525 miles)
Accommodation: Two seats side by side in enclosed cockpit. Dual controls standard. Cockpit heating optional
Construction: Braced wings of light alloy construction, with metal ribs and skins. Cambered wingtips of glassfibre. Light alloy tubular fuselage keel, to which glassfibre lower and upper fairings are attached. Optional vee-shaped stepped lower hull for amphibious operations. Twin-boom tail unit of light alloy. Non-retractable landing gear

History: Larkin Aircraft Corporation initiated the design of the prototype Model KC-3 Skylark in 1961; construction began in 1970 and the first flight was achieved on 8 June 1972. Emphasis was placed on producing a robust structure suitable for homebuilders, the primary skill necessary to build a Skylark being that of sheet metal riveting.
Plans and material kits are available to amateur constructors, who may also order from the company any part or parts which they consider beyond their ability to fabricate. By 1976 one Skylark had been constructed in addition to the prototype

For details: PO Box 66899, Scotts Valley, California 95066, USA.

Two-seat light aircraft

Power plant: One 67 kW (90 hp) Continental C90-14F flat-four engine
Wing span: forward 7.92 m (26 ft 0 in)
　　　　　rear　　6.00 m (19 ft 8¼ in)
Wing area, gross: forward 9.92m² (106.8 sq ft)
　　　　　rear　　7.43 m² (80.0 sq ft)
Length overall: 4.77 m (15 ft 7¾ in)
Height overall: 2.08 m (6 ft 10 in)
Weight empty: 360 kg (794 lb)
Max T-O weight: 600 kg (1,323 lb)
Max level speed at 305 m (1,000 ft): 109 knots (201 km/h; 125 mph)
Max cruising speed: 97 knots (180 km/h; 112 mph)
Max rate of climb at S/L: 275 m (900 ft)/min
Service ceiling: over 3,660 m (12,000 ft)
Range at econ cruising speed of 87 knots (161 km/h; 100 mph): 477 nm (885 km; 550 miles)
Accommodation: Two seats side by side in enclosed cabin. Baggage space aft of seats

Construction: Tandem wings of wooden construction, fabric covered. Welded steel tube fuselage structure, covered with light alloy to front of cabin and with fabric on rear portion, over spruce formers. Wooden tail unit, fabric covered. Non-retractable landing gear

History: M François Lederlin designed and built this light aircraft, which is based on the familiar Mignet 'Pou-du-Ciel' formula. Although derived from the Mignet HM-380 and designated 380-L, it retains little of the original design except for the wing arrangement. First flight was made on 14 September 1965, a restricted C of A being granted in the following month.

Plans of the 380-L, annotated in English and with both English and metric measurements, are available to amateur constructors, and several examples of the 380-L are being constructed. A feature of this aircraft is that the controls comprise a rudder bar for directional control and a stick, suspended from the roof of the cabin and free laterally, to control the incidence of the pivoted forward wing. A further lever, suspended from the roof, controls the long-span tab on the rear wing

For details: 2 rue Charles Peguy, 38-Grenoble, France.

(France)

LEFEBVRE MP.205 BUSARD

Single-seat racing monoplane

Data: Prototype Busard with 67 kW (90 hp) Continental engine, unless otherwise stated
Power plant: One 67 kW (90 hp) Continental flat-four engine
Wing span: 6.00 m (19 ft 8¼ in)
Wing area, gross: 6.00 m² (64.6 sq ft)
Length overall: Continental engine   5.35 m (17 ft 6¾ in)
Volkswagen engine   5.20 m (17 ft 0¾ in)
Height overall: 1.50 m (4 ft 11 in)
Weight empty: 239 kg (527 lb)
Max T-O weight: 345 kg (760 lb)
Max level speed at S/L:
Continental   156 knots (290 km/h; 180 mph)
Volkswagen (1,600 cc) 113 knots (210 km/h; 130 mph)
Range with max fuel (48.5 kW; 65 hp Continental): 242 nm (450 km; 279 miles)
Accommodation: Single seat in enclosed cabin. Baggage space aft of seat
Construction: Wooden wing structure, covered with plywood.

Fabric-covered wooden slotted ailerons and flaps. Conventional wooden fuselage structure, covered with plywood. Plastics engine cowling. Wooden tail structure, plywood and fabric covered. Non-retractable landing gear

History: M Robert Lefebvre built and flew this racing aircraft, assisted by pupils of the A. Camus technical school at Rouen. Basis of the design was the MP.204 prototype racer, with 56 kW (75 hp) Minie engine, designed by Max Plan and first flown on 5 June 1952. By comparison with the MP.204, the Busard has been lightened, and simplified for construction by amateurs. The prototype built by M Lefebvre was powered originally with a 48.5 kW (65 hp) Continental engine. After 20 flying hours it was re-engined with a 67 kW (90 hp) Continental and underwent further refinement, including the fitting of main-wheel fairings.

By early 1975 fifteen sets of plans had been sold to amateur constructors. One Busard is being built with a 48.5 kW (65 hp) Walter engine, two with versions of the Volkswagen, and the remainder with Continentals

For details: CES A. Camus, rue Adeline, 76100-Rouen, France.

Ganagobie with 27.5 kW (37 hp) Continental A40 engine

(Australia)

Single-seat light aircraft

Data: All-wood homebuilt version
Power plant: Designed for a modified Volkswagen engine of at least 26 kW (35 hp), with a direct-drive two-blade propeller; a typical engine is the Sportavia Limbach SL 1700 D. Alternatively, geared-down VW engines with either vee-belt or geared reduction drive may be installed, provided that the aircraft does not exceed its weight and CG range limitations
Wing span: 7.40 m (24 ft 3¼ in)
Wing area, gross: 8.57 m² (92.25 sq ft)
Length overall: 4.92m (16 ft 1¾ in)
Height overall: 1.83 m (6 ft 0 in)
Weight empty: 285 kg (630 lb)
Max T-O weight: 362 kg (800 lb)
Max level speed (with SL 1700 D engine): 98 knots (182 km/h; 113 mph)
Max cruising speed (75% power; engine as above): 87 knots (161 km/h; 100 mph)
Service ceiling: 3,050 m (10,000 ft)
Accommodation: Single seat in fully enclosed cabin
Construction: Braced wing of wooden construction, with non-structural plywood or aluminium leading-edge and fabric covering. Wooden basic fuselage structure, with plywood covering. Steel tube engine mounting and wing root cabane structure. Wooden tail unit, with plywood covered fixed surfaces and fabric covered movable surfaces. Non-retractable landing gear

History: The original Ganagobie was designed and built by the brothers William and James Lobet at Lille, France, and made its first flight in 1953, powered by an old Clerget engine. After modification and redesignation as Ganagobie 02, it flew for a further 30 hours before being grounded by engine failure in 1954, and later became Ganagobie 2 when fitted with a two-stroke target-drone engine. Further modifications were then incorporated.
The second aircraft, Ganagobie 3, was built in Canada by Mr La Rue Smith, powered by a 53.5 kW (72 hp) McCulloch engine. A later Ganagobie 3 was fitted with a 30 kW (40 hp) Continental engine and this version can also be powered with modified Volkswagen engines of 1,500 cc and above. The ultra-light Ganagobie 4 is suitable for 36 kW (48 hp) Nelson and other small two-stroke engines. Latest version of the aircraft is the Ganagobie 05, designed primarily for amateur construction and described in detail above. Construction of the basic homebuilt aircraft is all-wooden; but production versions are under consideration, to be marketed either in kit form with a fabric-covered steel tube fuselage and wooden wings and tail, or in factory-built form with fabric-covered metal wings and tail control surfaces
For details: Suite 7/506 Miller Street, 2062 – Cammeray, New South Wales 2062, Australia.

Single-seat lightweight sporting monoplanes

Data: S-20
Power plant: One 1,500 cc Volkswagen modified motor car engine, developing 39.5 kW (53 hp)
Wing span: 7.62 m (25 ft 0 in)
Wing area, gross: 8.73 m² (94 sq ft)
Length overall: 5.64 m (18 ft 6 in)
Height overall: 1.60 m (5 ft 3 in)
Weight empty: 206 kg (456 lb)
Design T-O weight: 326 kg (720 lb)
Max level speed, from S/L to 610 m (2,000 ft): 96 knots (177 km/h; 110 mph)
Max cruising speed, same heights as above: 78 knots (145 km/h; 90 mph)
Max rate of climb at S/L: 259 m (850 ft)/min
Range with max fuel, no reserve: 218 nm (404 km; 251 miles)
Accommodation: Single seat in open cockpit. Space for 9 kg (20 lb) of baggage aft of seat
Construction: All-metal construction. Non-retractable landing gear

History: The S-20 was designed to be simple to build, easy to fly and economical in operation. It is of all-metal construction, and fabrication is simplified by the extensive use of pop-rivets.
Design and construction of the prototype S-20 began simultaneously in March 1969. First flight was made on 9 March 1972. Since then the S-20 has been flown on one occasion from Sonoma, California, to the EAA Fly-in at Oshkosh, Wisconsin, a distance of 1,606 nm (2,977 km; 1,850 miles).
The designation S-20 applies only to the prototype. Aircraft built to Mr Robert MacDonald's plans have the designation S-21. Sales of plans totalled around 100 sets by early 1976, and the first aircraft to be built from them was expected to make its first flight during that year. Other S-21s were in an advanced stage of construction

For details: 1282 Fowler Creek Road, Sonoma, California 95476, USA.

S-20 version

(USA)

Single-seat eight-tenths scale replica biplane

Power plant: One 67 kW (90 hp) LeBlond 5F radial engine
Wing span, both: 7.62 m (25 ft 0 in)
Length overall: 6.71 m (22 ft 0 in)
Height overall: 2.44 m (8 ft 0 in)
Weight empty: 345 kg (762 lb)
Max T-O weight: 554 kg (1,222 lb)
Max level speed: 61 knots (113 km/h; 70 mph)
Cruising speed: 57 knots (105 km/h; 65 mph)
Max rate of climb at S/L: 122 m (400 ft)/min
Accommodation: Single seat in open cockpit

Construction: Braced wings with wooden structure, Dacron covered. Braced fuselage and tail unit structures of welded steel tube, Dacron covered. Non-retractable landing gear

History: Mr Joe Mason constructed this eight-tenths scale replica of a D.H.2 biplane fighter of First World War vintage. He created his own constructional drawings by reference to a three-view drawing in a 1965 magazine and as many illustrations as he could find. The project occupied a period of 8½ years, with the first flight on 1 March 1974, at a cost of approximately $4,500. Reduced scale was essential to permit construction of the aircraft in a garage

Single-seat sporting monoplane

Power plant: One 48.5 kW (65 hp) Continental flat-four engine
Wing span: 12.19 m (40 ft 0 in)
Wing area, gross: 13.38 m^2 (144.0 sq ft)
Length overall: 6.10 m (20 ft 0 in)
Height over tail: 1.60 m (5 ft 3 in)
Weight empty, equipped: 351 kg (775 lb)
Max T-O weight: 476 kg (1,050 lb)
Max level speed at S/L: 118 knots (219 km/h; 136 mph)
Normal cruising speed at 3,050 m (10,000 ft), (50% power): 109 knots (203 km/h; 126 mph)
Max rate of climb at S/L: 271 m (890 ft)/min
Service ceiling (computed): 7,315 m (24,000 ft)
Range at normal cruising speed at 3,050 m (10,000 ft), with

30 min reserves: 291 nm (540 km; 336 miles)
Accommodation: Single seat under one-piece bubble canopy
Construction: Wooden wing structure with plywood, glassfibre and fabric covering. Wooden fuselage structure with plywood and glass-fibre covering. Wooden tail structure with plywood and fabric covering. Retractable monowheel landing gear

History: The WM-2 is a low-powered, high-performance aircraft, conceived for the exploration of wave soaring conditions, thermal soaring with the engine stopped, and high-altitude, economical powered sport flying. The prototype was built by Mr William Miller between 1969 and 1972, and made its first flight in August 1972. Flight testing was undertaken during 1973-74, and plans have been prepared for amateur construction of the aircraft

For details: Box 570, RR1, Furlong, Pennsylvania 18925, USA.

Single-seat lightweight monoplane

Power plant: One 53.5 kW (72 hp) Revmaster Model 1831D modified Volkswagen motor car engine
Wing span: 5.49 m (18 ft 0 in)
Wing area, gross: 5.30 m² (57 sq ft)
Length overall: 4.04 m (13 ft 3 in)
Width overall, wings removed: 1.83 m (6 ft 0 in)
Height overall: 2.10 m (6 ft 10 in)
Weight empty: 238 kg (525 lb)
Max T-O weight: 362 kg (800 lb)
Max level speed, estimated: 152 knots (282 km/h; 175 mph)
Max cruising speed, estimated: 139 knots (257 km/h; 160 mph)
Max rate of climb at S/L, estimated: 274-305 m (900-1,000 ft)/min
Service ceiling, estimated: 3,050 m (10,000 ft)
Max range, estimated: 608 nm (1,126 km; 700 miles)

Accommodation: Single seat under transparent cockpit canopy
Construction: All-metal construction. Non-retractable landing gear

History: Mini-Hawk International was formed to market plans and kits for construction of the Tiger Hawk. Three officers of the company combined their efforts to design and construct the prototype, which made its first flight during 1974. The flight test programme was to be completed in 1976.

The Tiger Hawk features simplified construction and has easily-detachable wings for towing or storage. Removal of the wings takes only ten minutes. Mini-Hawk offers amateur constructors a complete set of plans and a construction manual, or a complete kit package with or without an engine

For details: 1930 Stewart Street, Santa Monica, California 90404, USA.

(USA)

Single-seat Formula V racing monoplane

Power plant: One 44.5 kW (60 hp) Volkswagen 1,600 cc modified motor car engine
Wing span: 5.08 m (16 ft 8 in)
Wing area, gross: 6.97 m² (75 sq ft)
Length overall: 5.08 m (16 ft 8 in)
Height overall: 1.52 m (5 ft 0 in)
Weight empty: 199 kg (440 lb)
Max T-O weight: 317 kg (700 lb)
Max level speed at S/L: over 139 knots (257 km/h; 160 mph)
Max cruising speed: 130 knots (241 km/h; 150 mph)
Range: over 260 nm (482 km; 300 miles)
Accommodation: Single seat under jettisonable Plexiglas bubble canopy
Construction: Conventional light alloy wing structure. Fuselage and tail unit of welded chrome-molybdenum steel tube construction, with fabric covering. Non-retractable landing gear

History: Mr John T. Monnett began design of the Sonerai in September 1970, construction starting two months later. First flight was made in July 1971, and FAA certification in the Experimental category has been granted. Known originally as the Monnett II Sonerai, the prototype received the 'Best in Class' Formula V Racer award at the EAA Fly-in at Oshkosh in 1971, as well as an award for its outstanding contribution to low-cost flying. Since that time a two-seat version of the Sonerai has been designed, with the result that the original model is now known as the Sonerai and the two-seat model (described separately) as the Sonerai II.

Plans and certain components are available to amateur constructors, including the glassfibre engine cowling, clear or tinted Plexiglas cockpit canopy, main landing gear struts, formed aluminium ribs, tapered-rod tail spring, fuel tanks, spar kits, instruments, injector carburettor, wheels and brakes.

By 1975 approximately 280 sets of plans had been sold and more than 100 Sonerais were known to be under construction

For details: 955 Grace, Elgin, Illinois 60120, USA.

(USA)

MONNETT SONERAI II

Two-seat high-performance sporting monoplane

Power plant: One 48.5-52 kW (65-70 hp) Volkswagen 1,700 cc modified motor car engine
Wing span: 5.69 m (18 ft 8 in)
Wing area, gross: 7.80 m² (84 sq ft)
Length overall: 5.74 m (18 ft 10 in)
Weight empty: 230 kg (506 lb)
Max T-O weight: 419 kg (925 lb)
Max level speed at S/L: approx 143 knots (266 km/h; 165 mph)
Max cruising speed at S/L: 122 knots (225 km/h; 140 mph)
Max rate of climb at S/L: 229 m (750 ft)/min
Range with max fuel and max payload, 30 min reserve: 364 nm (676 km; 420 miles)
Accommodation: Two seats in tandem beneath transparent bubble canopy

Construction: As for Sonerai

History: The success of the Sonerai (*which see*) encouraged initiation of the design and construction of a two-seat version in December 1972. Generally similar to the Sonerai, the Sonerai II differs by being slightly larger and by having a more powerful engine. It is stressed to ± 4.4*g* in the Utility category and ± 6*g* in the single-seat Aerobatic category.
The prototype made its first flight in July 1973, and by 1975 orders had been received for 225 sets of plans. Many components, complete kits for fuselage and wings, and materials, are also available to amateur constructors

For details: 955 Grace, Elgin, Illinois 60120, USA.

Single-seat ultra-light monoplanes

Power plant: Standard power plant is one 33.5 kW (45 hp) Rollason Ardem X flat-four engine. More powerful versions of the Ardem engine can be fitted

Wing span (without tip-tanks): 6.00 m (19 ft 8 in)

Wing span (with tip-tanks): 6.25 m (20 ft 6 in)

Wing area, gross: 7.50 m² (80.70 sq ft)

Length overall: 4.56 m (15 ft 0 in)

Height overall: 1.91 m (6 ft 3 in)

Weight empty: 210 kg (465 lb)

Max T-O weight: aerobatic 310 kg (685 lb)
normal 340 kg (750 lb)

Max level speed at S/L:
without tip-tanks 93 knots (173 km/h; 107 mph)
with tip-tanks 83 knots (155 km/h; 96 mph)

Max cruising speed (75% power) at S/L: without tip-tanks 81 knots (150 km/h; 93 mph)

Max rate of climb at S/L: 198 m (650 ft)/min

Service ceiling: 3,660 m (12,000 ft)

Range with tip-tanks: 390 nm (720 km; 450 miles)

Range with max internal fuel, 30 min reserve: 173 nm (320 km; 200 miles)

Accommodation: Single seat under blown Perspex canopy. Small baggage space aft of seat

Construction: Wooden wing structure, with plywood-covered leading-edge and overall fabric covering. Welded steel tube fuselage structure. Underfuselage fairing of glassfibre. Rear fuselage fabric-covered. Wooden tailplane and elevators. Steel tube rudder, fabric covered. Non-retractable landing gear

History: Complete worldwide rights for the Nipper aircraft were purchased from Belgium in 1966, and the aircraft was marketed in both factory-built form and as several stages of kits for amateur construction.

The former Nipper Aircraft Ltd went into receivership in May 1971; on 20 October 1971 a new company was formed, named Nipper Kits and Components Ltd, to supply spares for existing aircraft and to encourage and support amateur construction of the Nipper. Plans and an advisory service for amateur constructors continue to be available.

The Mk III Nipper is powered by a 1,500 cc Rollason Ardem engine; when fitted with a 1,600 cc Ardem engine the aircraft is known as the Mk IIIA

For details: 1 Ridgeway Drive, Bromley, Kent BR1 5DG, England.

Nipper Mk III with 33.5 kW (45 hp) Ardem X engine

(USA)

Single-seat light monoplane

Data: Performance figures for aircraft with 1,600 cc engine
Power plant: One 31.5 kW (42 hp) 1,600 cc or 30 kW (40 hp) 1,500 cc Volkswagen modified motor car engine
Wing span: 5.49 m (18 ft 0 in)
Width, wings detached: 1.83 m (6 ft 0 in)
Length overall: 3.91 m (12 ft 10 in)
Weight empty: 140 kg (310 lb)
Max T-O weight: 267 kg (590 lb)
Max level speed: 104 knots (193 km/h; 120 mph)
Max cruising speed (75% power): 95.5 knots (177 km/h; 110 mph)
Max rate of climb at S/L: 244 m (800 ft)/min
Service ceiling: 4,575 m (15,000 ft)
Range: 347 nm (643 km; 400 miles)
Accommodation: Single seat in open cockpit. Drawings of optional canopy available
Construction: All-metal construction. Non-retractable landing gear

History: This aircraft is an improved version of Mr Cal Parker's original Jeanie's Teenie, now known as Teenie One, of which several thousand sets of plans were sold. The original aim was to produce an aircraft specifically to utilise the Volkswagen motor car engine and, at the same time, to evolve an all-metal design that would present few constructional problems even to homebuilders with virtually no metal-working experience. This was achieved, and no special tools or jigs are needed to build the Teenie Two beyond a tool to close and form the cadmium-plated steel pop-rivets that are used for practically all assembly. One gauge of aluminium sheet and one size of light alloy angle section is used for virtually all of the structure, except for chromoly steel tube and sheet which are used for construction of the landing gear and control actuation tubes respectively. For simplicity and economy, push/pull tubes are used for all flying control circuits.

The Teenie Two, a considerably more refined and cleaner aircraft than the Teenie One, first flew in 1969. The prototype cost approximately $650 to build, over a period of six months. Its structure is stressed for full aerobatics, but the fuel and oil systems are not suitable for inverted flight. Although tested with various propellers, a computer-designed propeller is available in the parts kit which gives optimum performance for take-off, climb and cruise.

Plans, complete kits of parts, and details of how to modify Volkswagen engines are available to amateur constructors, and some Teenie Twos built from plans had completed 750 flying hours by early 1976. A two-seat version of the Teenie, named *Double Teenie*, is under construction

For details: PO Box 181, Dragoon, Arizona 85609, USA.

(USA)

Single-seat light biplane
Data: Version with 67 kW (90 hp) engine
Power plant: One 67 kW (90 hp) Continental C90 flat-four engine. Alternatively, any other Continental or Lycoming flat-four engine of 63.5-108 kW (85-145 hp)
Wing span: upper   4.57 m (15 ft 0 in)
              lower   3.96 m (13 ft 0 in)
Wing area, gross: 5.57 m² (60 sq ft)
Length overall: 4.27 m (14 ft 0 in)
Height overall: 1.60 m (5 ft 3 in)
Weight empty: 243 kg (535 lb)
Max T-O weight: 435 kg (960 lb)
Max level speed at S/L: 139 knots (257 km/h; 160 mph)
Max cruising speed: 122 knots (225 km/h; 140 mph)
Max rate of climb at S/L: 275 m (900 ft)/min
Range with max fuel: 338 nm (625 km; 390 miles)
Accommodation: Single seat, normally in open cockpit. Baggage compartment with 9 kg (20 lb) capacity
Construction: All-wood wing structure, plywood-covered and with fabric covering overall. Steel tube truss fuselage structure, with wood stringers and fabric covering. Vertical tail surfaces have fabric-covered steel tube structure; horizontal surfaces have plywood-covered wood structure, with fabric covering overall. Non-retractable landing gear

History: The original prototype of the Knight Twister KT-85 sporting biplane flew in 1933. Considerable refinement of the design since that time has improved both the appearance and the performance of later models, which have been built in substantial numbers by amateur constructors in the United States and elsewhere.

The most powerful Knight Twister flown to date is owned by Mr Charles Williams of Mount Prospect, Illinois, and has a 134 kW (180 hp) Lycoming O-360 engine installed. The recommended engines are noted above.

During 1971 Mr Payne modified the design of the tailplane, which now has increased span and reduced chord, the area remaining unchanged. Plans and kits of the Knight Twister KT-85 are available to amateur constructors. Three other versions exist; the Knight Twister Imperial with a new wing section, increased wing and tailplane span, increased fuel tankage, a 101 kW (135 hp) Lycoming O-290-D2 engine, and max speed of 156 knots (290 km/h; 180 mph); the Sunday Knight Twister SKT-125, with increased wing area, making it easier to fly; and the Knight Twister Junior KT-75 with tapered wings of larger area, a Continental or Lycoming engine of 56-93 kW (75-125 hp), and a max speed of 117 knots (217 km/h; 135 mph) with the 75 hp engine

For details: Route No 4, PO Box 319M, Escondido, California 92025, USA.

KT-85 with 119 kW (160 hp) Lycoming O-320-B engine

(USA)

PAZMANY PL-1 LAMINAR

Two-seat light aircraft

Power plant: one 71 kW (95 hp) Continental C90-12F flat-four engine
Wing span: 8.53 m (28 ft 0 in)
Wing area, gross: 10.78 m² (116 sq ft)
Length overall: 5.77 m (18 ft 11 in)
Height overall: 2.64 m (8 ft 8 in)
Weight empty, equipped: 363 kg (800 lb)
Max T-O weight: 602 kg (1,326 lb)
Max level speed at S/L: 104 knots (193 km/h; 120 mph)
Max cruising speed at S/L: 100 knots (185 km/h; 115 mph)
Max rate of climb at S/L: 305 m (1,000 ft)/min
Service ceiling: 5,500 m (18,000 ft)
Range with max fuel: 521 nm (965 km; 600 miles)
Accommodation: Two seats side by side under rearward-sliding transparent canopy. Dual controls.
Construction: All-metal construction. Non-retractable landing gear

History: A prototype Laminar, constructed by Mr John Green and

Mr Keith Fowler, was flown for the first time on 23 March 1962, the test pilots being Cdr Paul Hayek, USN, and Lieut Richard Gordon, who is best known as one of the Gemini/Apollo astronauts. Some 5,000 design hours and 4,000 hours of construction went into the prototype, which had logged more than 1,500 flying hours by January 1976.

Pazmany Aircraft Corporation is no longer marketing plans for the PL-1, but a total of 375 sets of plans and building instructions were sold prior to the decision to concentrate on the PL-2 (*which see*), and PL-1s are being built in the USA, Canada, Australia, Norway and other countries. In early 1968 the Aeronautical Research Laboratory of the Chinese Nationalist Air Force, at Taichung, Taiwan, acquired a set of PL-1 drawings. Under the supervision of General Ku and Colonel Lee, personnel of the ARL built a PL-1 in the record time of 100 days. It was flown for the first time on 26 October 1968 and on 30 October was presented to the late Generalissimo Chiang Kai-Shek. Extensive flight testing resulted in the decision to utilise the PL-1 as a basic trainer for CAF cadets, and 58 aircraft, designated PL-1B, were constructed between 1970 and 1974, each powered by a 112 kW (150 hp) Lycoming O-320 engine

(USA)

Two-seat light monoplane

Data: 93 kW (125 hp) version
Power plant: One Lycoming flat-four engine, including the 80.5 kW (108 hp) O-235-C1, 93 kW (125 hp) O-290-G (ground power unit), 101 kW (135 hp) O-290-D2B, or 112 kW (150 hp) O-320-A
Wing span: 8.53 m (28 ft 0 in)
Wing area, gross: 10.78 m² (116 sq ft)
Length overall: 5.90 m (19 ft 3½ in)
Height overall: 2.44 m (8 ft 0 in)
Weight empty: 408 kg (900 lb)
Max T-O weight: 655 kg (1,445 lb)
Max level speed at S/L: 125 knots (232 km/h; 144 mph)
Econ cruising speed: 111 knots (206 km/h; 128 mph)
Max rate of climb at S/L: 457 m (1,500 ft)/min
Range at econ cruising speed: 422 nm (780 km; 486 miles)
Accommodation: Two seats side by side in enclosed cabin
Construction: All-metal construction. Non-retractable landing gear

History: Plans of this aircraft are available to amateur constructors, and 276 sets had been sold by early 1975.

The PL-2 is almost identical externally to the PL-1, having been developed from the earlier aircraft. Cockpit width is increased by 5 cm (2 in) and wing dihedral is increased from 3° to 5°. The internal structure is extensively changed, to simplify construction and reduce weight.

Static tests of every major assembly up to ultimate loads had been made by early 1967. The first PL-2 to be completed was built by Mr H. Pio of Ramona, California, and this aircraft made its first flight on 4 April 1969, powered by the O-290-G engine. A single example of the PL-2 was built by the Vietnam Air Force, each VNAF base contributing towards its construction. This aircraft flew for the first time on 1 July 1971, and it was reported that production of at least ten more PL-2s was being considered, for use at the VNAF Air Training Center. Others have been built for testing and evaluation by the Royal Thai Air Force and the Republic of Korea Air Force, as well as one built in Japan by the Miyauchi Manufacturing Co Ltd and about 50 similar LT-200s built by 1976 in Indonesia by the Lipnur Aircraft Industry of Bandung. The first flight of an LT-200 took place on 9 November 1974

For details: Box 80051, San Diego, California 92138, USA.

(USA)

Single-seat lightweight sporting aircraft

Power plant: One 1,600 cc modified Volkswagen motor car engine with Becar V-belt reduction of 2¼:1, developing approximately 37.5 kW (50 hp)
Wing span: 8.13 m (26 ft 8 in)
Wing area, gross: 8.27 m² (89.0 sq ft)
Length overall: 5.04 m (16 ft 6½ in)
Height overall: 1.73 m (5 ft 8 in)
Weight empty: 262 kg (578 lb)
Max T-O and landing weight: 385 kg (850 lb)
Max level speed at S/L: 109 knots (201 km/h; 125 mph)
Max cruising speed at S/L: 85 knots (158 km/h; 98 mph)
Max rate of climb at S/L: 198 m (650 ft)/min
Service ceiling: 3,960 m (13,000 ft)
Range with max fuel, no allowances: 295 nm (545 km; 340 miles)
Accommodation: Single seat under transparent Plexiglas canopy, hinged on starboard side. Compartment aft of seat for 9 kg (20 lb) of baggage
Construction: All-metal construction. Non-retractable landing gear

History: The PL-4A was designed specifically for easy, low-cost construction by amateur builders, to provide a safe aircraft that would be economical in operation. The prototype, which first flew on 12 July 1972, had completed approximately 312 hours of flight by January 1976. Sets of plans, kits of prefabricated components, glassfibre wingtips and fuel tanks, and transparent cockpit canopies are available to amateur constructors.

By February 1976, approximately 500 sets of plans had been sold, and the PL-4A had received approval in Australia for construction by amateurs.

In November 1973, Lt Col Roy Windover, Director of the Air Cadets Programme, Canadian Ministry of Defence, made a flight evaluation of the PL-4A prototype. As a result of this, it is planned to provide 200 of these aircraft for the Air Cadets. Two pre-production aircraft are being built to evaluate two different power plant installations. The first of these aircraft was expected to be completed during 1976. Components for the pre-production aircraft, as well as the production version, are being made by inmates of a civil prison, who are responsible also for assembly of the first two aircraft. The remainder will be assembled by Air Cadets, who will use them for cross-country, aerobatic and IFR flying

For details: Box 80051, San Diego, California 92138, USA.

Lightweight sporting monoplane

Power plant: One converted 1,385 cc Volkswagen motor car engine, producing 30 kW (40 hp)
Wing span, with cambered wingtips: 6.71 m (22 ft 0 in)
Wing area, gross, with cambered wingtips: 6.34 m² (68.25 sq ft)
Length overall: 4.42 m (14 ft 6 in)
Height overall: 1.27 m (4 ft 2 in)
Weight empty: 154 kg (340 lb)
Max T-O weight: approx 254-272 kg (560-600 lb)
Max level speed at S/L: 69 knots (129 km/h; 80 mph)
Max cruising speed at S/L: 61 knots (113 km/h; 70 mph)
Max rate of climb at S/L: 152 m (500 ft)/min
Service ceiling: 3,050 m (10,000 ft)
Accommodation: Single seat in open position
Construction: Braced wing of composite construction, with wooden spars, polyurethane foam ribs and sheet foam skins, covered with Dynel fabric and impregnated with epoxy resin. Basic fuselage structure consists of light alloy square-section tubes.

Non-retractable landing gear

History: The PDQ-2 was designed to provide a cheap, robust, easily and quickly built aircraft that would be easy for an average pilot to fly. Design began in September 1972, and construction was started on 5 January 1973. Excluding the engine, the cost of construction was only $350, and the first flight was made on 30 May 1973. During 1975 it became obvious that an alternative power plant was needed, as supplies of the Rockwell (Venture) JLO-LB-600-2 two-cylinder engine fitted to the prototype were becoming scarce. Although one amateur constructor was reported to be powering his aircraft with a BMW motorcycle engine, it was decided to test the prototype with a Volkswagen engine. Although this increased the empty weight, the engine proved satisfactory during test flights, and the results of the tests are being relayed to all those interested in the aircraft. Plans of the PDQ-2 have been sold to amateur constructors in over 30 countries

For details: 28975 Alpine Lane, Elkhart, Indiana 46514, USA.

(USA)

Two-seat lightweight amphibian

Power plant: One 112 kW (150 hp) Lycoming O-320 flat-four engine
Wing span: 7.92 m (26 ft 0 in)
Wing area, gross: 12.08 m² (130 sq ft)
Length overall: 6.25 m (20 ft 6 in)
Height overall (wheels down): 1.83 m (6 ft 0 in)
Weight empty: 440 kg (970 lb)
Max T-O weight: 707 kg (1,560 lb)
Never-exceed speed: 130 knots (241 km/h; 150 mph)
Max cruising speed (75% power): 113 knots (209 km/h; 130 mph)
Max rate of climb at S/L: 365 m (1,200 ft)/min with pilot only
Accommodation: Two seats side by side beneath transparent canopy. Dual controls. Baggage compartment with 41 kg (90 lb) capacity.
Construction: Wooden structure, plywood covered except for wing aft of main spar, which is fabric covered. Hull undersurface contours formed from polyurethane foam, protected with glassfibre, as are the wingtip floats. Retractable wheel landing gear

History: Osprey Aircraft was formed originally to market the Osprey I. This was an unusual project for the homebuilder, being a flying-boat that was intended for operation on and from enclosed waters rather than the open sea. The plans included drawings of a special trailer for carriage of the aircraft, which allowed the pilot to launch and recover the Osprey unassisted.

On 27 July 1971, the US Navy purchased the prototype, under the designation X-28A Air Skimmer, to study the potential of a small single-seat seaplane for civil police duties in Southeast Asia.
Design and construction of the Osprey II, a two-seat amphibian development of the Osprey I, began in January 1972. Mr Pereira evolved an unusual form of hull construction for this aircraft. When the all-wood fuselage structure had been completed and the controls installed, the undersurface was given a deep coating of polyurethane foam. This was then sculptured to the requisite hull form, before being covered with several protective layers of glass-fibre cloth bonded with resin. The resulting structure is light, but extremely strong, with good shock resisting characteristics.
First flight of the Osprey II from water was made in April 1973, the amphibian becoming airborne in less than 244 m (800 ft). In later tests from land it was found that, with the landing gear retracted and at a speed of about 104 knots (193 km/h; 120 mph), there was slight buffet aft of the cabin and that the noise level was unacceptably high. Modifications made in early 1974 included lengthening the cabin by 0.18 m (7 in), and installation of a Lycoming O-320 engine in place of the original Franklin Sport, in a new cowling. Testing was resumed and completed satisfactorily during 1974, since when the shape of the tail fin has been changed. Sets of plans are available to amateur constructors

For details: 3741 El Ricon Way, Sacramento, California 95825, USA.

(UK)

Single-seat ultra-light monoplane

Data: D31 Turbulent with 33.5 kW (45 hp) engine
Power plant: One 33.5 kW (45 hp) Rollason Ardem 4CO2 Mk IV (Volkswagen conversion), or one 41 kW (55 hp) Ardem Mk V flat-four engine
Wing span: 6.58 m (21 ft 7 in)
Wing area, gross: 7.20 m^2 (77.5 sq ft)
Length overall: 5.33 m (17 ft 6 in)
Height overall: 1.52 m (5 ft 0 in)
Weight empty: 179 kg (395 lb)
Max T-O weight: 281 kg (620 lb)
Max level speed: 95 knots (176 km/h; 109 mph)
Max cruising speed: 87 knots (161 km/h; 100 mph)
Max rate of climb at S/L: 137 m (450 ft)/min
Service ceiling: 2,740 m (9,000 ft)
Range with max fuel, normal allowances: 217 nm (400 km; 250 miles)
Accommodation: Single seat in open cockpit. Sliding canopy available as optional extra. Baggage locker aft of seat, capacity 11.5 kg (25 lb)
Construction: All-wood structure, fabric covered except for fuselage and fixed tail surfaces which are plywood covered. Non-retractable landing gear

History: This aircraft operates with a Special Category C of A and plans are available to amateur constructors through the Popular Flying Association.

The original D31 Turbulent was designed by the late Roger Druine, a Frenchman who had designed and built his first aircraft in 1938 at the age of seventeen. He died in 1958. In 1957, Rollason Aircraft and Engines Ltd acquired a licence to build the Druine Turbulent, and also manufactured components of this aircraft to assist homebuilders. The first Rollason-built Turbulent flew on 1 January 1958, and 30 had been built by January 1974.

Rollason built a slightly modified Turbulent which was awarded a full C of A in 1966. Only major modification was an improved wing main spar; but the D31As intended for C of A approval also had to be fitted with a CAA-approved 1,500 cc Ardem Mk X engine, developing 33.5 kW (45 hp). Three D31As had been built by 1974; but the manufacture of Turbulents and components by Rollason ended in 1975. Responsibility for the Turbulent in the UK is now vested in the Popular Flying Association, which markets plans for this aircraft to amateur constructors

For details: Terminal Building, Shoreham Airport, Shoreham-by-Sea, Sussex BN4 5FF, England.

(UK)

Single-seat light monoplane
Data: Performance data for Minor with Aeronca-JAP J.99 engine (27.5 kW; 37 hp)
Power plant: One aircooled engine in the 27.5-41 kW (37-55 hp) range
Wing span: 7.62 m (25 ft 0 in)
Wing area, gross: 11.6 m² (125 sq ft)
Length overall: 6.32 m (20 ft 9 in)
Height overall: 2.29 m (7 ft 6 in)
Weight empty: 177 kg (390 lb)
Max T-O weight: 340 kg (750 lb)
Max level speed at 457 m (1,500 ft): 60 knots (111 km/h; 69 mph)
Max rate of climb at S/L: 76 m (250 ft)/min
Range with standard fuel: 155 nm (290 km; 180 miles)
Accommodation: Single seat in open cockpit. Coupé top optional. Baggage space aft of seat
Construction: Wooden structure, fabric covered except for wing leading-edges and tips, and sides and bottom of fuselage, which are plywood covered. Non-retractable landing gear

History: Following the closure of Phoenix Aircraft Ltd, the Popular Flying Association has assumed responsibility for marketing plans of the Luton L.A.4a Minor.

The first Luton Minor flew in 1936 and proved entirely suitable for construction and operation by amateur builders and pilots. Examples were built pre-war in England and other parts of the world. In 1960, the design was modernised and re-stressed completely, to the latest British Airworthiness Requirements, allowing for a power increase to 41 kW (55 hp) and a maximum flying weight of 340 kg (750 lb). By December 1969, 149 sets of plans for the Minor had been sold. Minors are under construction in many parts of the world, and several amateur-built examples have been completed and flown successfully since mid-1962. At least one of them, built in Australia, has obtained a full Certificate of Airworthiness

For details: Terminal Building, Shoreham Airport, Shoreham-by-Sea, Sussex BN4 5FF, England

(France)

Two-seat aerobatic monoplane

Data: Dimensions, weights and performance figures for the C.P.750 unless stated otherwise
Power plant: One 48.5 kW (65 hp) Continental C65-8F flat-four engine in the C.P.70. One 112 kW (150 hp) Lycoming O-320-E2A flat-four engine in the C.P.750
Wing span: 8.04 m (26 ft 4½ in)
Wing area, gross: 11.00 m² (118 sq ft)
Length overall: 6.90 m (22 ft 7¾ in)
Height overall: 2.10 m (6 ft 10¾ in)
Weight empty: 480 kg (1,058 lb)
Max T-O weight: 760 kg (1,675 lb)
Max level speed:
    C.P.750   151 knots (280 km/h; 174 mph)
    C.P.70   95 knots (175 km/h; 109 mph)
Max cruising speed (75% power) at 1,200 m (3,940 ft):
    C.P.750   143 knots (265 km/h; 165 mph)
Max rate of climb at S/L:
    C.P.750   390 m (1,280 ft)/min
    C.P.70   120 m (394 ft)/min
Service ceiling:
    C.P.750   5,200 m (17,050 ft)
    C.P.70   3,000 m (9,850 ft)

PIEL C.P.70 and C.P.750 BERYL

Range at econ cruising speed of 135 knots (250 km/h; 155 mph):
    C.P.750 593 nm (1,100 km; 683 miles)
Range at econ cruising speed of 78 knots (145 km/h; 90 mph):
    C.P.70 323 nm (600 km; 372 miles)
Accommodation: Two seats in tandem under rearward-sliding transparent canopy. Rear seat of C.P.70 is wide enough to accommodate one adult and a child, or two children
Construction: Wooden wing structure, fabric covered. Wooden (C.P.70) or welded steel tube (C.P.750) fuselage structure, fabric covered. Wooden tail structure, plywood and fabric covered. Non-retractable landing gear

History: The prototype of the C.P.70 Beryl light aircraft was displayed publicly for the first time in August 1965. It retains the wing of the C.P.30 Emeraude virtually unchanged, combining it with a modified fuselage and non-retractable tricycle landing gear.
Intended for aerobatic flying, the C.P.750 Beryl is also similar in general appearance to the Emeraude but has a longer fuselage, slightly reduced span, a non-retractable tailwheel-type landing gear and other changes. The C.P.750 has so far been built principally by amateur constructors in Canada, but may also be built in France, through facilities offered by M Choisel at Abbeville

For details: 104 Côte de Beulle, 78580-Maule, France.

(France)

PIEL C.P.80/ZEF

Single-seat racing monoplane

Data: Version with 67 kW (90 hp) engine
Power plant: One 67 kW (90 hp) Continental C90-8F flat-four engine. Provision for other engines, including a 48.5 kW (65 hp) Continental
Wing span: 6.00 m (19 ft 8¼ in)
Wing area, gross: 6.20 m² (66.7 sq ft)
Length overall: 5.30 m (17 ft 4¾ in)
Height overall: 1.70 m (5 ft 7 in)
Weight empty: 260 kg (573 lb)
Max T-O weight: 380 kg (837 lb)
Max level speed: 167 knots (310 km/h; 193 mph)
Max cruising speed (75% power) at 1,200 m (3,950 ft): 151 knots (280 km/h; 174 mph)
Max rate of climb at S/L: 720 m (2,360 ft)/min
Service ceiling: 6,000 m (19,685 ft)

Range at econ cruising speed of 130 knots (240 km/h; 149 mph): 243 nm (450 km; 280 miles)
G **limits:** +8*g*; −6*g*
Accommodation: Single seat, in enclosed cockpit, under sideways-hinged transparent canopy
Construction: Wooden structure, plywood covered, with polyester plastics wingtips and engine cowling. Non-retractable landing gear

History: The C.P.80 was designed as a racing monoplane for amateur construction. The basic structure is normally of wood, but M Calvel of l'Hospitalet du Larzac adapted the design to enable his Zef to be constructed of laminated plastics. This was the first C.P.80 Zef to fly, followed in July 1974 by the C.P.80 Racer No. 01 built by M Claude Piel.
About 20 wooden C.P.80s are under construction by amateurs.

For details: 104 Côte de Beulle, 78580-Maule, France.

Three/four-seat and two-seat light monoplanes respectively

Data: C.P.301 Emeraude
Power plant: One 67 kW (90 hp) Continental C90-12F flat-four engine
Wing span: 8.04 m (26 ft 4½ in)
Wing area, gross: 10.85 m² (116.7 sq ft)
Length overall: 6.30 m (20 ft 8 in)
Height overall: 1.85 m (6 ft 0¾ in)
Weight empty: 380 kg (838 lb)
Max T-O weight: 650 kg (1,433 lb)
Max level speed: 110 knots (205 km/h; 127 mph)
Max cruising speed (75% power) at 1,200 m (3,940 ft): 108 knots (200 km/h; 124 mph)
Max rate of climb at S/L: 168 m (551 ft)/min
Service ceiling: 4,000 m (13,125 ft)
Range at 101 knots (187 km/h; 116 mph): 538 nm (1,000 km; 620 miles)
Accommodation: Two seats side by side in enclosed cockpit. Dual controls. Heating and ventilation
Construction: Wooden structure, fabric covered. Non-retractable landing gear

History: There have been several factory-built versions of the Emeraude and Super Emeraude, but the aircraft are no longer being produced in this form. The designs continue to be available for amateur construction, and the following amateur-built versions have flown: C.P.301 as above; C.P.302 with 67 kW (90 hp) Salmson engine; C.P.303 with 63.5 kW (85 hp) Salmson engine; C.P.304 with 63.5 kW (85 hp) Continental C85-12F engine and wing flaps; C.P.305 with 86 kW (115 hp) Lycoming engine; C.P.308 with 56 kW (75 hp) Continental engine; C.P.320 with Super Emeraude wings and 74.5 kW (100 hp) Continental engine; C.P.320A with swept-back fin; C.P.321 as for C.P.320 but with 78.5 kW (105 hp) Potez engine; C.P.323A with 112 kW (150 hp) Lycoming engine and sweptback fin; and C.P.323AB with tricycle landing gear.

The Emeraude is one of the types approved by the Popular Flying Association for amateur construction in the United Kingdom.

The Diamant is essentially a three/four-seat version of the Emeraude. It is fully certificated for commercial production and is available in plan form for amateur construction. The C.P.60, C.P.601 and C.P.602 versions, with engines in the 67-86 kW (90-115 hp) range, are no longer built. Current versions are as follows: C.P.604 Super Diamant, first flown as prototype in 1964, with 108 kW (145 hp) Continental engine – Current version has swept vertical tail surfaces; C.P.605 Super Diamant, a much-modified 2+2 version with 112 kW (150 hp) Lycoming O-320-E2A engine, fully certificated for commercial production as well as for amateur construction; and C.P.605B Super Diamant, similar to C.P.605 but with retractable tricycle landing gear

For details: 104 Côte de Beulle, 78580-Maule, France.

Super Diamant

Single-seat sporting biplane

Power plant: One 134 kW (180 hp) Lycoming IO-360-B4A flat-four engine
Wing span, upper: 5.28 m (17 ft 4 in)
Wing area, gross: 9.15 m² (98.5 sq ft)
Weight empty: 326 kg (720 lb)
Max T-O weight: 521 kg (1,150 lb)
Max level speed at S/L: 153 knots (283 km/h; 176 mph)
Max cruising speed at S/L: 122 knots (227 km/h; 141 mph)
Max rate of climb at S/L: 816 m (2,675 ft)/min
Service ceiling: 6,795 m (22,300 ft)
Range with max fuel, no reserve: 273 nm (507 km; 315 miles)
Accommodation: Single seat in open cockpit
Construction: Wooden wing structure, fabric covered. Welded steel tube fuselage and tail structures, fabric covered. Non-retractable landing gear

History: The original single-seat Pitts Special was designed in 1943-44. Construction of the prototype began in 1944 and it flew for the first time in September of that year. Since then, increasingly powerful engines have been installed in single-seat and two-seat Pitts Specials, examples of which have been flown with outstanding success by US and British competitors in the World Aerobatic Championships, as well as by aerobatic formations such as the famous Rothmans team in the UK. The S-1D version of the aircraft is intended solely for homebuilders, and plans are available to amateur constructors. By early 1976 about 300 S-1s were under construction or flying

For details: PO Box 548, Homestead, Florida 33030, USA.

(USA)

POWELL P-70 ACEY DEUCY

Two-seat monoplane

Data: Performance figures relate to prototype
Power plant: Suitable for installation of engines from 48.5-67 kW (65-90 hp). Prototype has one 48.5 kW (65 hp) Continental A65 flat-four engine
Wing span: 9.91 m (32 ft 6 in)
Wing area, gross: 14.4 m² (155 sq ft)
Length overall: 6.32 m (20 ft 9 in)
Height overall: 2.06 m (6 ft 9 in)
Weight empty: 340 kg (750 lb)
Max T-O weight: 578 kg (1,275 lb)
Max level speed at 305 m (1,000 ft): 85 knots (158 km/h; 98 mph)
Max cruising speed at 305 m (1,000 ft): 72 knots (134 km/h; 83 mph)
Max rate of climb at S/L: 107-137 m (350-450 ft)/min
Range with max fuel, 7.5 litres (2 US gallons) reserve: 217 nm (402 km; 250 miles)

Accommodation: Two seats in tandem in open cockpits
Construction: Braced composite wing structure of steel tube and wood, fabric covered. Welded steel tube fuselage structure with wooden stringers, fabric covered. Braced tail unit of welded steel tube construction. Non-retractable landing gear

History: John Powell, formerly a Commander in the US Navy, designed and built this parasol-wing monoplane, of which plans are available to amateur constructors. Its design was started in 1966, and construction began during 1967. FAA certification in the Experimental (homebuilt) category was awarded on 19 June 1970, and the first flight was recorded on the following day. By the beginning of 1976 the prototype had accumulated 535 hours' flying time. More than 80 sets of plans have been sold, and the first aircraft built from plans was flying by the Autumn of 1973. It is believed that about 25 more Acey Deucys are either flying or under construction

For details: 4 Donald Drive, Middleton, Rhode Island 02840, USA.

(USA)

RAND ROBINSON KR-1 and KR-2

Single-seat (KR-1) and two-seat (KR-2) lightweight sporting monoplanes

Data: KR-1 with 27 kW (36 hp) engine
Power plant: One 1,700 cc Volkswagen modified motor car engine, developing 43 kW (58 hp), now fitted to prototype; most aircraft have a 1,200 cc Volkswagen engine of 27 kW (36 hp). The KR-2 has an airframe designed to accept Volkswagen engines of between 1,600 and 2,200 cc
Wing span: 5.23 m (17 ft 2 in)
Wing area, gross: 5.95 m^2 (64 sq ft)
Length overall: 3.81 m (12 ft 6 in)
Height overall: 1.07 m (3 ft 6 in)
Weight empty, equipped: 154 kg (340 lb)
Max T-O weight: 272 kg (600 lb)
Max level speed at S/L: 130 knots (241 km/h; 150 mph)
Max cruising speed at 1,525 m (5,000 ft): 130 knots (241 km/h; 150 mph)
Max rate of climb at S/L: 182 m (600 ft)/min
Service ceiling: 3,660 m (12,000 ft)
Range with max fuel: 650 nm (1,203 km; 748 miles)
Accommodation: Pilot only, beneath transparent cockpit canopy. Small baggage hold
Construction: Composite wing structure, with front spar of spruce, rear spar of spruce and plywood. Most ribs formed from Styrofoam plastics; spaces between them filled with Styrofoam slab. Structure covered with Dynel epoxy. Composite fuselage structure, lower half of spruce and plywood, upper part of carved Styrofoam covered with Dynel epoxy. Tail unit of spruce and carved Styrofoam, Dynel epoxy covered. Retractable landing gear

History: During 1974 Mr Rand formed Rand Robinson Engineering Inc to market plans for the KR-1 and the two-seat KR-2. Earlier, he had designed and built the prototype of the single-seat version, which was known originally as the Rand KR-1. The design originated in 1969; construction was started in 1970, and the first flight was made in February 1972. The prototype was subsequently re-engined, as noted above, giving it a max speed of 174 knots (322 km/h 200 mph) and a range of 2,600 nm (4,825 km; 3,000 miles). About 5,770 sets of plans had been sold by early 1976, and about 200 KR-1s are flying.

The KR-2 is a slightly larger two-seat version of the KR-1, to which it is generally similar in construction. Design began in 1973 and the prototype flew for the first time in July 1974. Construction occupied about 800 man-hours, at a cost of about $2,000. Plans and kits of parts are available to amateur constructors. By March 1976, a total of 2,030 sets of plans and 1,000 kits had been sold; about 100 KR-2s were flying by 1976

For details: 5842 K McFadden Avenue, Huntington Beach, California 92649, USA.

KR-1 version

(Canada)

Single-seat sporting biplane

Power plant: Various engines can be installed; performance figures quoted below are for aircraft with a 63.5 kW (85 hp) Continental C-85 engine
Wing span: 6.96 m (22 ft 10 in)
Wing area, gross: 13.01 m² (140 sq ft)
Height overall: 2.18 m (7 ft 2 in)
Weight empty: 358 kg (790 lb)
Max T-O weight: 499 kg (1,100 lb)
Max level speed at S/L: 78 knots (145 km/h; 90 mph)
Max cruising speed: 74 knots (137 km/h; 85 mph)
Max rate of climb at S/L: 152 m (500 ft)/min
Accommodation: Single seat in open cockpit
Construction: Wooden wing structure; leading edge covered with glassfibre or aluminium, remainder fabric. Ply-skinned box fuselage structure, with fabric covered turtledeck and aluminium covered

REPLICA PLANS SE-5A REPLICA

forward top section. Wooden tail structure with similar covering to wings. Non-retractable landing gear

History: The SE-5A Replica was designed as an easy to build and inexpensive representation of the famous First World War fighter, although exact reproduction was waived in favour of making the aircraft simple to construct, using modern materials.
Design began in 1969, in which year construction of the first prototype also started. The SE-5A prototypes were fitted with Continental engines ranging from 48.5-74.5 kW (65-100 hp) although larger engines can be installed in the aircraft to the individual homebuilder's preference. The first prototype flew in 1970, and certification was granted by the FAA in the Experimental (homebuilt) category.
Plans are available to amateur builders and by April 1976 about 209 sets had been sold

For details: 953 Kirkmond Crescent, Richmond, B.C., Canada.

Two-seat light helicopter

Power plant: One RotorWay horizontally-opposed engine, designed and produced for the Scorpion Too
Diameter of main rotor: 7.32 m (24 ft 0 in)
Length, nose to tail rotor axis: 6.18 m (20 ft 3½ in)
Height to top of main rotor: 2.22 m (7 ft 3 ½ in)
Width of cabin: 1.22 m (4 ft 0 in)
Weight empty: 340 kg (750 lb)
Max T-O weight: 544 kg (1,200 lb)
Cruising speed: 74-78 knots (136-145 km/h; 85-90 mph)
Max rate of climb at S/L: 244 m (800 ft)/min
Service ceiling: 3,050 m (10,000 ft)
Range, standard fuel (approx): 104 nm (193 km; 120 miles)
Accommodation: Two individual bucket seats side-by-side in enclosed cabin
Construction: Two-blade semi-rigid main rotor, incorporating Schramm Tractable Control rotor system. Basic steel tube fuselage structure of simplified form. Removable glassfibre body fairings.

Braced steel tube tailboom, to carry tail rotor. Tubular skid type landing gear

History: Mr B.J. Schramm formed a company to market, in both ready-to-fly and prefabricated component form, a single-seat helicopter of his design named the Javelin. Subsequently, a new company named RotorWay Inc was set up to market to amateur constructors, plans and kits of components to build the Scorpion helicopter, described as a production version of the Javelin. The company has now ended production of this helicopter, which has been superseded by a two-seat version known as the Scorpion Too. RotorWay offers comprehensive plans, technical advice from its engineers, a preflight training school, a complete kit to build the helicopter, or a series of small progressive kits, allowing the constructor to proceed as finance allows. The company will also supply plans and rotor blades to those builders wishing to provide their own materials and engine

For details: 14805 S. Interstate 10, Tempe, Arizona 85281, USA.

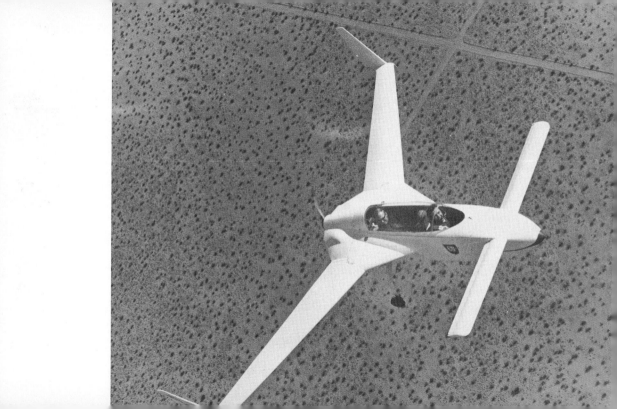

Two-seat sporting aircraft

Power plant: One 74.5 kW (100 hp) Continental O-200 flat-four engine in second prototype
Wing span: 6.81 m (22 ft 4 in)
Wing area, gross: 4.98 m² (53.6 sq ft)
Foreplane span: 4.03 m (13 ft 2½ in)
Length overall: 3.79 m (12 ft 5 in)
Weight empty: 222 kg (490 lb)
Max T-O weight: 444 kg (980 lb)
Max cruising speed: 181 knots (335 km/h; 208 mph)
Econ cruising speed: 126 knots (233 km/h; 145 mph)
Max rate of climb at S/L: 549 m (1,800 ft)/min
Range (75% power): 608 nm (1,126 km; 700 miles)
Range at econ cruising speed: 955 nm (1,770 km; 1,100 miles)
Accommodation: Two semi-reclining seats in tandem in individual cockpits, under one-piece bubble canopy. Space for 14 kg (30 lb) of baggage
Construction: Wings and foreplane of unidirectional glassfibre, with rigid urethane foam core. Composite fuselage structure, comprising large sheets of rigid urethane foam, with wood strips as corner fillers, and internal and external covering of unidirectional glassfibre. Light alloy extrusion used for engine and landing gear mounts, etc. Non-retractable main landing gear; retractable nosewheel

History: The name VariEze stems from this aircraft's simplicity of construction. Its configuration is based on that of the VariViggen but differs mainly in having more conventional swept wings of high aspect ratio, each tip carrying a vertical fin or 'winglet' based on the latest NASA aerodynamic research.

Designed in late 1974, the VariEze was built over a ten-week period in the Spring of 1975 and made its first flight on 21 May. Optimum economy cruise performance was a primary design aim, so that the prototype could be used to attack existing world distance records in the under-500 kg gross weight class C1a. (It has been reported that on 4 August 1975 the aircraft set a new world's closed-circuit distance record in this Class). A second aircraft was built during the Winter of 1975/76, incorporating some modifications compared with the original VariEze. This latter aircraft became the prototype for the homebuilding programme, and is powered by a Continental O-200 engine instead of the first aircraft's 47 kW (63 hp) 1,834 cc Volkswagen modified motor car engine. However, homebuilt aircraft can be constructed with VW engines of 1,600 cc to 1,834 cc capacity. By early 1976 the first VariEze had completed approximately 220 flying hours.

Plans and certain components are available to homebuilders. The latter include the Plexiglas canopy, moulded glassfibre nosewheel and main landing gear struts, glassfibre cowling, moulded urethane foam centre bulkhead/seat assembly, a three-piece wing spar/centre-section spar system which permits removal of each wing after withdrawal of a single retaining pin, and the engine mounting, as well as all raw materials

For details: PO Box 656, Mojave Airport, Mojave, California 93501, USA.

Two-seat light aircraft

Power plant: One 112 kW (150 hp) Lycoming O-320-A2A flat-four engine
Wing span: 5.79 m (19 ft 0 in)
Wing area, gross: 11.06 m² (119 sq ft)
Foreplane span: 2.44 m (8 ft 0 in)
Length overall: 5.79 m (19 ft 0 in)
Weight empty, equipped: 431 kg (950 lb)
Max T-O and landing weight: 771 kg (1,700 lb)
Max level speed at S/L: 142 knots (262 km/h; 163 mph)
Max cruising speed at 2,135 m (7,000 ft): 130 knots (241 km/h; 150 mph)
Max rate of climb at S/L: 366 m (1,200 ft)/min
Service ceiling: 4,265 m (14,000 ft)
Range with max fuel, 30 min reserve: 347 nm (643 km; 400 miles)
Accommodation: Two seats in tandem in individual cockpits, beneath transparent canopies. Space for 45 kg (100 lb) of baggage
Construction: Composite wing structure, with spruce spars, plywood ribs and skins, all Ceconite-covered, except for outboard aft wing panels which are of flush-riveted metal construction. Wooden fuselage structure, Ceconite covered. Retractable landing gear

History: The prototype of a new light aircraft named the VariViggen was rolled out on 27 February 1972. Mr Burt Rutan had begun its design in 1963 and the configuration had been developed via a low-cost automobile-mounted test system. This involved construction of a one-fifth scale model, which was mounted on a specially-built test rig attached to the roof of a motor car. Ailerons, rudders and canard elevators on the model were operated by remote control; transducers in the test rig allowed measurement of airspeed, angle of attack, lift, drag, sideslip, side force, roll moment and elevator/aileron/rudder position. An extra data channel provided for measurement of stick forces and structural load.

Construction of the prototype VariViggen began in 1968, and first flight was made in May 1972. By early 1976 this aircraft had accumulated a total of nearly 600 flying hours. It displays no conventional stall, and can climb, cruise, glide turn and land with continuous full aft stick, with a stable speed of 45 knots (84 km/h; 52 mph) throughout.

In 1975 Mr Rutan began experimenting with a new wing outer panel of increased span, constructed from urethane foam and unidirectional glassfibre. It was anticipated that this would provide a 25% increase in the max rate of climb and offer a slightly better cruising speed. A second VariViggen is also under construction by Mr Rutan.

Plans are available to amateur constructors; over 500 sets have been sold, and it is thought that approximately 245 aircraft are being built

For details: PO Box 656, Mojave Airport, Mojave, California 93501, USA.

Two-seat sporting or aerobatic biplane

Power plant: Prototype has one 134 kW (180 hp) Lycoming O-360-A3A flat-four engine. Installation designed to take Lycoming engines of 112-149 kW (150-200 hp)

Wing span: upper 6.10 m (20 ft 0 in)
           lower   5.79 m (19 ft 0 in)

Wing area, gross: 13.75 m² (148 sq ft)

Length overall: 5.79 m (19 ft 0 in)

Weight empty: 388 kg (856 lb)

Max T-O weight: 612 kg (1,350 lb)

Cruising speed (75% power) at 1,525 m (5,000 ft): 130 knots (241 km/h; 150 mph)

Max rate of climb at S/L: 915 m (3,000 ft)/min

Service ceiling: 4,570 m (15,000 ft)

Range with max fuel: 325 nm (603 km; 375 miles)

Accommodation: Two seats in tandem in individual cockpits. Space for 9 kg (20 lb) of baggage

Construction: Braced wooden wing structure, fabric covered. Welded steel tube fuselage structure, fabric covered. Braced steel tube and wood tail unit, fabric covered. Non-retractable landing gear

History: Mr William Shober designed, built and flew the prototype of this sporting biplane, which he named the Willie II. Being stressed for a loading of ±9g, the aircraft is suitable for limited aerobatics in standard homebuilt configuration. The plans which are available to amateur constructors give details of the necessary fuel system conversions to make Willie II capable of inverted flight. The designer estimates that 2,500 to 3,000 hours of work are involved in building the aircraft

For details: PO Box 111, Gaithersburg, Maryland 20760, USA.

(USA)

SIEGRIST RS1 ILSE

Four-seat cabin monoplane

Power plant: One 134 kW (180 hp) Lycoming O-360 flat-four engine
Wing span: 8.53 m (28 ft 0 in)
Wing area, gross: 12.36 m² (133 sq ft)
Length overall: 6.55 m (21 ft 6 in)
Height overall: 1.91 m (6 ft 3 in)
Weight empty: 532 kg (1,173 lb)
Max T-O weight: 943 kg (2,080 lb)
Max level speed at S/L: 148 knots (274 km/h; 170 mph)
Cruising speed (60% power): 130 knots (241 km/h; 150 mph)
Accommodation: Four seats in enclosed cabin. Cabin heated and ventilated
Construction: Braced wooden wings, with plywood skin, covered overall with glassfibre and epoxy resin. Ailerons and flaps of metal construction. Welded steel tube fuselage structure, with wood stringers; light alloy skin around cockpit area and glassfibre covering on the remainder. Welded steel tube tail unit, covered with glassfibre. Non-retractable landing gear

History: This design originated in 1965. Construction of the prototype began in 1966 and the first flight was made in June 1971. FAA certification in the Experimental category was awarded in August of the same year. While en route from California, in July 1973, at which time the RS1 had completed approximately 180 flight hours, two-thirds of one propeller blade sheared off in flight. A successful forced landing caused no further damage, but the violent vibration before the engine was shut down had sheared many engine mounting tubes. Before the aircraft was put back into airworthy condition, a new engine mount was designed, differing from the original, to provide space between engine and firewall to mount a governor for a constant-speed propeller.

Plans for the RS1 Ilse were delayed by this incident, but were 80% complete in 1975. The prototype was expected to fly again in 1976

For details: 6451 Myrtle Hill, Valley City, Ohio 44280, USA.

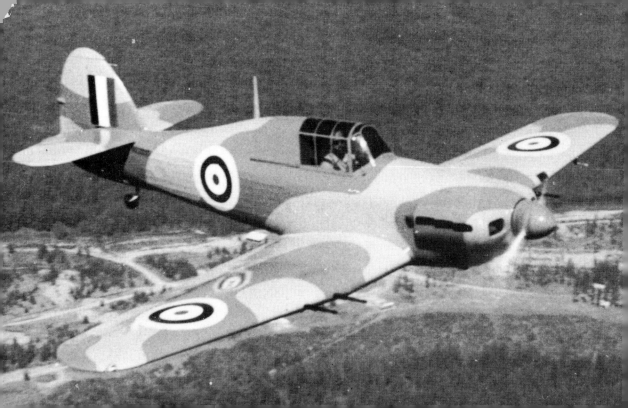

(USA)

Single-seat sporting monoplane

Power plant: One 112 kW (150 hp) Lycoming O-320 flat-four engine
Wing span: 7.62 m (25 ft 0 in)
Wing area, gross: 9.38 m² (101 sq ft)
Length overall: 5.99 m (19 ft 8 in)
Height overall: 1.78 m (5 ft 10 in)
Weight empty: 456 kg (1,005 lb)
Max T-O weight: 624 kg (1,375 lb)
Max level speed at S/L: 174 knots (322 km/h; 200 mph)
Max cruising speed (65% power) at 1,830 m (6,000 ft): 143 knots (265 km/h; 165 mph)
Max rate of climb at S/L: 564 m (1,850 ft)/min
Max range, no reserve fuel: 542 nm (1,005 km; 625 miles)
Accommodation: Single seat beneath rearward-sliding canopy. Cockpit heated and ventilated. Space for 18 kg (40 lb) of baggage aft of pilot's seat .

SINDLINGER HH-1 HAWKER HURRICANE

Construction: Wooden structure, fabric covered overall. Retractable landing gear

History: Mr Fred G. Sindlinger began the design of this ⅝-scale replica of the Second World War Hawker Hurricane IIC fighter in April 1969. Construction of the prototype was started three months later, and the first flight was made in January 1972. By February 1973, Mr Sindlinger's Hurricane had accumulated approximately 160 flying hours, and a full stress analysis of the aircraft had been completed.
Plans and certain component parts were made available to amateur constructors from September 1973. By January 1976 about 30 sets had been sold and approximately 12 aircraft were under construction, including examples being built in Africa, Australia and Germany

For details: 5923 9th Street NW, Puyallup, Washington 98371, USA.

Single-seat sporting biplane

Power plant: Designed to take any engine in 48.5-93 kW (65-125 hp) category. Prototype has 80.5 kW (108 hp) Lycoming O-235-C flat-four engine

Wing span: upper 5.18 m (17 ft 0 in)

            lower 4.80 m (15 ft 9 in)

Wing area, gross: 9.29 m² (100 sq ft)

Length overall: 4.65 m (15 ft 3 in)

Height overall: 1.52 m (5 ft 0 in)

Weight empty, equipped: 279 kg (616 lb)

Max T-O weight: 454 kg (1,000 lb)

Max level speed at S/L: 117 knots (217 km/h; 135 mph)

Max cruising speed: 102 knots (190 km/h; 118 mph)

Max rate of climb at S/L: 380 m (1,250 ft)/min

Service ceiling: 3,960 m (13,000 ft)

Endurance with max fuel: 2 hr 30 min

Accommodation: Single seat in open cockpit. Space for 27 kg (60 lb) of baggage

Construction: Braced wooden wing structure, fabric covered. Welded steel tube fuselage and tail unit, fabric covered. Non-retractable landing gear

History: The late Frank W. Smith built and flew in October 1956 the prototype of a single-seat fully-aerobatic sporting biplane which he designated the DSA-1 (Darn Small Aeroplane) Miniplane. Plans of this aircraft continue to be marketed by Mrs Smith and some 350 sets have been sold to constructors in several countries. Apart from America, two are known to be flying in France, one in West Germany and others in Sweden and England. A two-seat version of the Miniplane has been designed by Mrs Smith's son and is provisionally designated Miniplane +1

For details: Mrs F. W. Smith, 3502 Sunny Hills Drive, Norco, California 91760, USA.

Two-seat sporting monoplane

Power plant: Provision for installation of engines from 67-134 kW (90-180 hp). Prototype has a 93 kW (125 hp) Lycoming O-290-G flat-four engine
Wing span: 7.57 m (24 ft 10 in)
Wing area, gross: 8.92 m² (96 sq ft)
Length overall: 5.89 m (19 ft 4 in)
Height overall: 1.66 m (5 ft 5½ in)
Weight empty: 393 kg (867 lb)
Max T-O and landing weight: 657 kg (1,450 lb)
Max level speed at 610 m (2,000 ft): 161 knots (298 km/h; 185 mph)
Max cruising speed (75% power) at 610 m (2,000 ft): 139 knots (257 km/h; 160 mph)
Max rate of climb at S/L, 0° C (32° F): 366 m (1,200 ft)/min
Service ceiling: 4,570 m (15,000 ft)
Range with max fuel, no reserve: 369 nm (684 km; 425 miles)
Accommodation: Two seats side by side under rearward-sliding bubble canopy. Compartment for 41 kg (90 lb) of baggage. Cabin heated and ventilated
Construction: All-metal construction. Non-retractable landing gear on prototype; retractable gear can be fitted

History: In February 1958 Mr Smyth began the design of a sporting monoplane, aiming to produce an aircraft that would be reasonably easy to build, easy to fly, stressed to 9*g* for limited aerobatics, and economical in operation. Construction of the prototype began in January 1967, and it took two years to build, at a cost of around $2,500. First flight of this aircraft, named Model 'S' Sidewinder, was made on 21 February 1969, and it received the Outstanding Design' award at the 17th EAA Fly-in in 1969.
Construction of the prototype was simplified by utilising a number of standard and readily-obtainable items of equipment. Plans are now available to amateur constructors, and Mr Smyth can also supply a glassfibre nosewheel fairing and two-piece engine cowling to those constructors who do not wish to mould their own

For details: PO Box 308, Huntington, Indiana 46750, USA.

Two-seat aerobatic biplane

Power plant: One 134 kW (180 hp) Lycoming O-360-B1E flat-four engine
Wing span: 6.96 m (22 ft 10 in)
Length overall: 6.35 m (20 ft 10 in)
Height overall: 1.80 m (5 ft 10¾ in)
Weight empty: 561 kg (1,236 lb)
Max T-O weight: 867 kg (1,911 lb)
Max level speed: 149 knots (277 km/h; 172 mph)
Max cruising speed at S/L: 139 knots (257 km/h; 160 mph)
Max rate of climb at S/L: 457 m (1,500 ft)/min
Service ceiling, estimated: 6,100 m (20,000 ft)
Range: 436 nm (807 km; 502 miles)
Accommodation: Two seats side by side in enclosed cabin. Dual controls standard. Baggage capacity 36 kg (80 lb). Cabin heated and ventilated

Construction: Braced wooden wing structure, fabric covered. Conventional steel-tube fuselage structure, fabric covered. Braced steel tube tail unit. Non-retractable landing gear

History: Sorrell Aviation designed and built this biplane with the intention of making it suitable for amateur construction. Design began in 1964, and construction of the first prototype was started in June 1971. This aircraft made its initial flight in March 1973; the second prototype, of developed form, first flew exactly two years later. When demonstrated and displayed at the EAA 1973 Fly-in at Oshkosh, it received the 'Outstanding New Design' award.
Plans are not sold separately, but a basic kit package, with construction drawings and certain completed components, is available to amateur constructors
For details: Box 660, Route 1, Tenino, Washington 98589, USA

Four-seat amphibian

Power plant: One 212 kW (285 hp) Continental Tiara series 6-285-B flat-six engine (*see History*)
Wing span: 11.38 m (37 ft 4 in)
Wing area, gross: 17.1 m² (184 sq ft)
Length overall: 8.05 m (26 ft 5 in)
Height overall: 2.90 m (9 ft 6 in)
Weight empty: 993 kg (2,190 lb)
Max T-O weight: 1,451 kg (3,200 lb)
Max level speed at S/L: 128 knots (237 km/h; 147 mph)
Max cruising speed at 1,675 m (5,500 ft): 122 knots (225 km/h; 140 mph)
Max rate of climb at S/L: 305 m (1,000 ft)/min
Range (65% power) at 2,375 m (7,800 ft), 20 min reserve: 695 nm (1,285 km; 800 miles)
Accommodation: Four seats in pairs in enclosed cabin. Rear seats fold back against bulkhead to provide cargo or baggage space. Further baggage space in rear fuselage. Dual controls standard. Accommodation heated and ventilated
Construction: Braced wing of wood, steel and glassfibre. Glass-fibre stabilising floats. Conventional hull, with wood frames, longe-rons and skin. Welded steel tube cabane structure, to provide wing and engine mounting and attachment points for landing gear. Retractable landing gear

History: Mr P.H. Spencer received a patent for his basic Air Car configuration on 3 January 1950. The original version was a two-seat amphibian powered by an 82 kW (110 hp) engine, and was developed into a four-seat version, known as the S-12-C. Mr Spencer then completed the design of the more advanced S-12-D, of which plans are available to homebuilders, as well as certain glassfibre mouldings and metal assemblies. Development has continued, and the installation of a Teledyne Continental Tiara 6-285-B engine has resulted in a change of designation to S-12-E for the prototype. This had accumulated a total of 750 hours' flying time by early 1976, 370 of them with the Tiara engine. The wing sweepback has also been increased

By early 1976 a total of 25 Air Cars were known to be under construction, with a variety of power plants ranging from 149 to 212 kW (200-285 hp), and 110 sets of plans had been sold. About 8 or 9 Air Cars were expected to make their maiden flights during 1976

For details: 8725 Oland Avenue, Sun Valley, California 91352, USA.

Two-seat sporting monoplane

Power plant: One 112 kW (150 hp) Lycoming O-320 flat-four engine
Wing span: 7.55 m (24 ft 9 in)
Wing area, gross: 11.21 m² (120.7 sq ft)
Length overall: 5.56 m (18 ft 3 in)
Height overall: 1.57 m (5 ft 2 in)
Weight empty: 408 kg (900 lb)
Max T-O weight: 680 kg (1,500 lb)
Max level speed at S/L: 130 knots (241 km/h; 150 mph)
Cruising speed: 109-117 knots (201-217 km/h; 125-135 mph)
Max rate of climb at S/L: 732 m (2,400 ft)/min
Endurance with max fuel: 3 hr
Accommodation: Two seats in tandem in open cockpits. Small baggage compartment
Construction: Strut-braced wing of wooden construction, fabric covered. Steel tube fuselage structure, with wood or light alloy stringers and fabric covering. Braced tail unit of steel tube construction, fabric covered. Non-retractable landing gear

History: Mr and Mrs Spezio designed and built the prototype of this two-seat, open-cockpit (hence Tuholer) light aircraft, of which all rights were acquired by Mr William Edwards in August 1973. He is continuing to market plans of the Tuholer to amateur constructors. The prototype flew for the first time on 2 May 1961. Folding wings enable the aircraft to be kept in a normal home garage, and it can be towed behind a car on its own landing gear. It can be made ready for flight by two people in about 10 minutes, or by one person in 20 minutes

For details: 25 Madison Avenue, Northampton, Massachusetts 01060, USA.

Two-seat lightweight flying-boat

Power plant: One 59.5 kW (80 hp) Mercury '800' modified outboard two-stroke marine engine, driving a two-blade plastics pusher propeller through an extended drive-shaft
Wing span: 7.32 m (24 ft 0 in)
Wing area, gross: 8.92 m² (96 sq ft)
Length overall: 5.18 m (17 ft 0 in)
Height overall: 1.52 m (5 ft 0 in)
Weight empty: 226 kg (500 lb)
Max T-O weight: 453 kg (1,000 lb)
Accommodation: Two seats side by side, in open cockpit
Construction: Braced and pivoted controllable parasol wing of reinforced plastics construction. Hull structure of polyurethane foam, with reinforced plastics skin. Butterfly-type tail unit of reinforced plastics. No landing gear other than hull

History: Mr George Spratt has completed more than 30 years' work on developing a two-piece movable-wing control system, which is claimed to provide improved safety factors compared with a conventional aileron, elevator and rudder control system. In brief, the flying controls are so arranged that the wings are allowed to move freely and collectively in incidence, while their incidence is controlled differentially by a steering wheel. The wings' angle of attack can be adjusted by a separate control.

While working for Consolidated Vultee, Mr Spratt designed a roadable aircraft which featured an earlier version of his wing control system, but this did not enter production. Since that time he has concentrated on perfecting his idea as a private venture.

To flight test his movable-wing control system, Mr Spratt built a lightweight experimental flying-boat which was constructed mostly of plastics. Following this, he designed and constructed a more advanced prototype known as the Model 107. Mr Spratt claims that the Model 107 will neither stall nor spin, and displays 75% less reaction to turbulence than a conventional design. Plans of the aircraft are available to amateur constructors, and by early 1976 nearly 60 sets had been sold. The first amateur-built Model 107 flew for the first time in the latter part of 1975. Others were expected to fly by mid-1976

For details: PO Box 351, Media, Pennsylvania 19063, USA.

Two-seat aerobatic biplane

Data: 134 kW (180 hp) Lycoming-engined version
Power plant: One 134 kW (180 hp) Lycoming HO-360-B1B flat-four engine. Provision for alternative engines of 93-224 kW (125-300 hp)
Wing span: upper   7.32 m (24 ft 0 in)
            lower   7.01 m (23 ft 0 in)
Wing area, gross: 14.2 m² (152.7 sq ft)
Length overall: 5.79 m (19 ft 0 in)
Height overall: 2.13 m (7 ft 0 in)
Weight empty: 490 kg (1,080 lb)
Max T-O weight: 762 kg (1,680 lb)
Max level speed: 126 knots (233 km/h; 145 mph)
Cruising speed: 113 knots (209 km/h; 130 mph)
Max rate of climb at S/L: 762 m (2,500 ft)/min
Service ceiling: 5,500 m (18,000 ft)
Range with max fuel: 390 nm (720 km; 450 miles)

Accommodation: Two seats in open cockpits. Space for 13.6 kg (30 lb) of baggage
Construction: Braced wings of wooden construction, fabric covered. Welded chrome-molybdenum steel tube fuselage and tail unit, fabric covered. Non-retractable landing gear

History: Mr Lamar Steen designed this two-seat fully-aerobatic biplane with simplicity of construction as a primary aim. The prototype was built as a class project in a Denver, Colorado, high school, where Mr Steen is an aerospace teacher. Design began in mid-1968 and construction on 19 August 1969, costing approximately $5,000. The first flight of the Skybolt was made in October 1970. Stressed to +12 and −10*g*, the prototype received an EAA award for Best School Project. Plans are available to amateur constructors and well over 1,000 sets have been sold

For details: 3218 S Cherry Street, Denver, Colorado 80222, USA.

Skybolt with 149 kW (200 hp) Lycoming IO-360 engine

Single-seat aerobatic monoplane

Data: Model A has fuel system for prolonged inverted flight. Model B has both fuel and oil systems so modified and can also have a constant-speed propeller
Power plant: One 134 kW (180 hp) Lycoming AIO-360-A1A flat-four engine
Wing span: 7.47 m (24 ft 6 in)
Wing area, gross: A   8.73 m² (94 sq ft)
                       B   9.29 m² (100 sq ft)
Length overall: 5.82 m (19 ft 1 in)
Height overall: 1.73 m (5 ft 8 in)
Weight empty: A   385 kg (850 lb)
                  B   431 kg (950 lb)
Max T-O weight: A   544 kg (1,200 lb)
                    B   589 kg (1,300 lb)
Max level speed at 610 m (2,000 ft): 148 knots (274 km/h; 170 mph)
Max cruising speed at 610 m (2,000 ft): 139 knots (257 km/h; 160 mph)
Max rate of climb at S/L: 1,220 m (4,000 ft)/min
Service ceiling: 6,705 m (22,000 ft)
Range with max fuel: 303 nm (563 km; 350 miles)

Accommodation: Single seat under rearward-sliding bubble canopy. Large window in undersurface, forward of control column. Model B has also a quarter window in each side of the fuselage, beneath the wings
Construction: Wooden wings, with ailerons of wood, steel and fabric construction. Welded steel tube fuselage structure, with Ceconite covering. Braced tail unit of welded steel tube construction, fabric covered. Non-retractable landing gear

History: This aircraft was designed by Mr C.L. Stephens specifically for homebuilders who wish to take part in competitive aerobatics. The prototype, designated Model A, was designed for Margaret Ritchie, US National Women's Aerobatic Champion in 1966. The second aircraft, the Model B, was built for Dean S. Engelhardt of California.
First US aircraft known to be designed around the Aresti Aerocriptografic System for competitive aerobatics, the Akro is stressed to $+12g$ and $-11g$. Design of the Model A started in July 1966 and construction of the prototype began a month later. First flight of this version was made on 27 July 1967, and of the Model B on 9 July 1969.
Plans of the Akro are available to amateur constructors

For details: PO Box 3171, Rubidoux, California 92509, USA.

Akro with 149 kW (200 hp) Lycoming engine

Single-seat light monoplane

Power plant: One 27 kW (36 hp) modified Volkswagen 1,192 cc motor car engine
Wing span: 8.61 m (28 ft 3 in)
Wing area, gross: 10.3 m² (110.95 sq ft)
Length overall: 5.41 m (17 ft 9 in)
Height overall: 1.68 m (5 ft 6 in)
Weight empty: 198 kg (437 lb)
Max T-O weight: 317 kg (700 lb)
Max level speed at S/L: 69.5 knots (129 km/h; 80 mph)
Cruising speed: 65 knots (121 km/h; 75 mph)
Max rate of climb at S/L: 122 m (400 ft)/min
Absolute ceiling: 3,355 m (11,000 ft)
Endurance with max fuel, no reserve: 2½ hours
Accommodation: Single seat in open or enclosed cockpit. Provision for 4.5 kg (10 lb) of baggage
Construction: Strut-braced high wing of wooden construction (with steel tube compression members), fabric covered. Welded steel tube fuselage and tail unit, fabric covered. Non-retractable landing gear

History: Designed by Mr Donald Stewart and built in only five months, the prototype Headwind flew for the first time on 28 March 1962.

A new wing was designed for the Headwind during 1969, and this became an integral part of the plans available to homebuilders. In 1970, further modifications were made to the aircraft's fuselage, tail unit and landing gear, after which it was given the current JD₁ HW 1.7 designation. All the changes are included in the current plans and have been made available to all holders of earlier plans.

The power plant of the prototype Headwind embodies a belt-driven propeller reduction drive designed by Mr Stewart. Known as the Maximizer, this unit was put into production in 1972 and is available to amateur constructors for use with Volkswagen power plants.

Several thousand sets of plans for the Headwind have been sold. Over 150 aircraft are believed to be under construction, and approximately 15 are flying. A two-seat version of the Headwind was under construction in 1976

For details: 11420 Route 165, Salem, Ohio 44460, USA.

Headwind with 39.5 kW (53 hp) Volkswagen engine

(USA)

STEWART JD₂FF F00 FIGHTER

Single-seat lightweight sporting biplane

Power plant: One 93 kW (125 hp) Franklin Sport 4 flat-four engine. Provision for Lycoming engine of up to 112 kW (150 hp)
Wing span (both): 6.30 m (20 ft 8 in)
Wing area, gross: 13.0 m² (140 sq ft)
Length overall: 5.72 m (18 ft 9 in)
Height overall: 2.13 m (7 ft 0 in)
Weight empty: 328 kg (725 lb)
Max T-O weight: 499 kg (1,100 lb)
Max cruising speed: 100 knots (185 km/h; 115 mph)
Max rate of climb at S/L: 366 m (1,200 ft)/min
Accommodation: Single seat in open cockpit. Space for 4.5 kg (10 lb) of baggage
Construction: Braced wings of conventional construction, with wooden spars and light alloy ribs, fabric covered. Lower wing extends below the fuselage, where it is attached to a cabane, and is faired over with thin-gauge light alloy sheet. Welded steel tube fuselage structure, with wood formers and stringers, fabric covered. Braced tail unit of welded steel tube construction, fabric covered. Non-retractable landing gear

History: Design of the Foo Fighter began in October 1967, and the first prototype made its maiden flight in June 1971 powered by a six-cylinder Ford Falcon motor car engine developing 89.5 kW (120 hp) at 3,800 rpm. This engine was replaced subsequently by a 93 kW (125 hp) Franklin Sport 4.
A second prototype, similarly powered with a Franklin, was sold for exhibition flights by Lafayette Escadrille '76 in Pennsylvania. During 1972, Mr Stewart designed new wings for the Foo Fighter, of increased span and chord (as above). Since that time he has further modified the design to allow installation of Lycoming engines, and has made refinements to the fuselage, tail unit and landing gear. Sets of plans of the Foo Fighter are available to amateur constructors

For details: 11420 Route 165, Salem, Ohio 44460, USA.

(USA)

Two-seat sporting biplane

Data: Apply to the radial-engined Starduster Too built by Mr Jack Mills of Indiana

Power plant: One Warner Super Scarab engine of 123 kW (165 hp)

Wing span (upper): 7.32 m (24 ft 0 in)

Length overall: 6.10 m (20 ft 0 in)

Height overall: 2.29 m (7 ft 6 in)

Weight empty: 501 kg (1,105 lb)

Max T-O weight: 748 kg (1,650 lb)

Max level speed: 156 knots (290 km/h; 180 mph)

Cruising speed: 104 knots (193 km/h; 120 mph)

Max rate of climb at S/L: 792 m (2,600 ft)/min

Absolute ceiling: 3,050 m (10,000 ft)

Range: 260 nm (482 km; 300 miles)

Accommodation: Two seats in tandem in open cockpits

STOLP SA-300 STARDUSTER TOO

Construction: Wooden wing structure, fabric covered. Welded steel tube fuselage and tail unit structures, fabric covered. Glass-fibre turtleback. Non-retractable landing gear

History: Mr Louis A. Stolp and Mr George M. Adams designed and built a light sporting biplane known as the Starduster, which flew for the first time in November 1957; and founded Stolp Starduster Corporation to market plans, components and basic materials to amateur constructors. Plans for the original SA-100 single-seat Starduster are no longer available, but the company continues to market plans, kits and materials for the SA-300 Starduster Too, which is an enlarged two-seat version and is suitable for engines of 93-194 kW (125-260 hp). The prototype SA-300 was powered by a Lycoming O-360-A1A flat-four engine (134 kW; 180 hp)

For details: 4301 Twining, Riverside, California 92509, USA.

Single-seat parasol-wing monoplane

Data: Prototype
Power plant: Can be fitted with engines of 63.5-93 kW (85-125 hp), the 80.5 kW (108 hp) Lycoming being recommended. Prototype has a 1,500 cc Volkswagen modified motor car engine
Wing span: 7.62 m (25 ft 0 in)
Wing area, gross: 7.71 m² (83 sq ft)
Length overall: 5.18 m (17 ft 0 in)
Height overall: 2.03 m (6 ft 8 in)
Max T-O weight: 340 kg (750 lb)
Cruising speed: 78 knots (145 km/h; 90 mph)
Accommodation: Single seat in open cockpit
Construction: Wooden wing structure, Dacron covered. Welded steel tube fuselage structure, Dacron covered. Braced tail unit of welded steel tube construction, Dacron covered. Non-retractable landing gear

History: Construction of the prototype Starlet took only three months and cost $1,500. The first flight was made on 1 June 1969. Plans, kits and materials are available to amateur constructors.

For comparison with the prototype, the following performance figures apply to a Starlet built by Mr J.D. Hiller of Montgomery, Ohio. This differs from the standard plans in having a two-piece cantilever spring main landing gear, and is powered by a 74.5 kW (100 hp) Continental O-200-A engine. Mr Hiller's Starlet has a max level speed of 116 knots (216 km/h; 134 mph) and a max cruising speed of 103 knots (192 km/h; 119 mph). Max rate of climb at S/L is 404 m (1,325 ft)/min; service ceiling is 3,350 m (11,000 ft); and range is 304 nm (563 km; 350 miles) with 11.4 litres (3 US gallons) of reserve fuel. Empty weight is 347 kg (766 lb) and max T-O weight 499 kg (1,100 lb)

For details: 4301 Twining, Riverside, California 92509, USA.

Single-seat aerobatic biplane
Data: Prototype with original engine
Power plant: Prototype had originally one 149 kW (200 hp) Lycoming flat-four engine, but was re-engined with a 134 kW (180 hp) engine. Design is able to accept engines of 93-149 kW (125-200 hp)
Wing span, upper: 5.79 m (19 ft 0 in)
Wing area, gross: 9.75 m² (105 sq ft)
Length overall: 4.80 m (15 ft 9 in)
Height overall: 1.91 m (6 ft 3 in)
Weight empty: 335 kg (740 lb)
Max T-O weight: 539 kg (1,190 lb)
Aerobatic T-O weight: 476 kg (1,050 lb)
Max level speed (aerobatic weight): 156 knots (290 km/h; 180 mph)
Cruising speed (aerobatic weight): 143 knots (266 km/h; 165 mph)
Max rate of climb at S/L (aerobatic weight): more than 914 m (3,000 ft)/min

Endurance at cruising speed (aerobatic weight), with reserve: 2 hours
Accommodation: Single seat in open cockpit. Space for 23 kg (50 lb) of baggage in turtledeck compartment
Construction: Braced wings of wooden construction, fabric covered. All-metal fuselage and tail unit structures of light alloy. Non-retractable landing gear

History: Introduced in 1973, the SA-700 is fully aerobatic. Ailerons on both wings produce a roll rate in excess of 240° a second, and an interesting design feature is that the four ailerons are raised slightly when the control column is pulled back. This helps to maintain aileron control when the aircraft is stalled in a normal attitude. Conversely, the ailerons are drooped slightly when the control column is pushed forward, which helps to maintain aileron control in an inverted stall.
Plans and kits of components are available to amateur constructors
For details: 4301 Twining, Riverside, California 92509, USA.

Single-seat ultra-light monoplane
Power plant: One 28.3 kW (38 hp) JAP two-cylinder engine in prototype (*see also History*)
Wing span: 6.40 m (21 ft 0 in)
Wing area, gross: 7.06 m² (76 sq ft)
Length overall: 4.57 m (15 ft 0 in)
Height over tail: 1.47m (4 ft 10 in)
Weight empty: 186 kg (410 lb)
Max T-O weight: 276 kg (610 lb)
Max level speed at S/L: 91 knots (169 km/h; 105 mph)
Econ cruising speed: 78 knots (145 km/h; 90 mph)
Max rate of climb at S/L: 305 m (1,000 ft)/min
Range: 200 nm (370 km; 230 miles)
G limits: +9; −9
Accommodation: Single seat under transparent Perspex canopy. Aerobatic harness. Small locker aft of seat
Construction: All-wood structure with plywood covering, except for elevators and rudder which are fabric covered, and wings which are plywood and fabric covered. Non-retractable landing gear

History: The late Mr John Taylor designed and built the prototype of this sporting monoplane, designated J.T.1. His object was to produce the airframe for not more than £100. Construction took about 14 months, and the aircraft flew for the first time on 4 July 1959.
Plans of the Taylor Monoplane have been sold to amateur constructors in the United Kingdom and nearly 20 other countries. Forty-eight J.T.1s are known to be flying, including 11 in the UK, 9 in Canada, 19 in the USA, 4 in Australia, and 5 in New Zealand.
Aircraft currently flying or under construction are fitted with a variety of engines, including the 30 kW (40 hp) Aeronca E 113, 48.5 kW (65 hp) Continental A65, 48.5 kW (65 hp) Lycoming, 53.5 kW (72 hp) McCulloch, and modified Volkswagen engines

For details: 25 Chesterfield Crescent, Leigh-on-Sea, Essex SS9 5PD, England.

Single-seat light monoplane

Data: Basically for the prototype
Power plant: One 63.5 kW (85 hp) Continental C85 flat-four engine (*see also History*)
Wing span: 5.72 m (18 ft 9 in)
Wing area, gross: 6.32 m² (68 sq ft)
Length overall: 4.91 m (16 ft 1½ in)
Height overall: 1.42 m (4 ft 8 in)
Weight empty: 227 kg (500 lb)
Max T-O weight: 338 kg (745 lb)
Max level speed: 174 knots (322 km/h; 200 mph)
Normal cruising speed: 135 knots (250 km/h; 155 mph)
Max rate of climb at S/L: 335 m (1,100 ft)/min
Accommodation: Single seat under bubble canopy. Aerobatic harness
Construction: Wooden wing structure, plywood and fabric covered. Wooden fuselage structure, plywood covered, with aluminium cockpit and side panels. Wooden tail structure; fixed surfaces plywood covered and control surfaces fabric covered. Non-retractable landing gear

History: Construction of the prototype Titch was started in February 1965 and it flew for the first time on 22 January 1967. It had previously won second prize in the Midget Racer Design Competition organised by Mr Norman Jones of the Rollason company in 1964. The prototype crashed on 16 May 1967, killing its designer. However, Mrs J.F. Taylor is continuing to market plans for this successful aircraft to amateur constructors.
Fourteen Titches are known to be flying, including 8 in the USA, 2 in New Zealand, 1 in France, 1 in Rhodesia, and 2 in the UK; plans have been supplied also to amateur constructors in Brazil, Iceland, Italy, Mexico and Spain

For details: 25 Chesterfield Crescent, Leigh-on-Sea, Essex SS9 5PD, England.

(USA)

THORP T-18 TIGER

Two-seat high-performance sporting monoplane

Data: Standard aircraft, powered by a 134 kW (180 hp) Lycoming engine
Power plant: One Lycoming or Continental flat-four engine in the 80.5-149 kW (108-200 hp) category
Wing span: 6.35 m (20 ft 10 in)
Wing area, gross: 8.0 m² (86 sq ft)
Length overall: 5.54 m (18 ft 2 in)
Height overall: 1.47 m (4 ft 10 in)
Weight empty: 408 kg (900 lb)
Max T-O weight: 683 kg (1,506 lb)
Max level speed at S/L: 174 knots (321 km/h; 200 mph)
Max cruising speed: 152 knots (282 km/h; 175 mph)
Max rate of climb at S/L: 610 m (2,000 ft)/min
Service ceiling: 6,100 m (20,000 ft)
Range with max fuel: 434 nm (805 km; 500 miles)
Accommodation: Two seats side by side in open cockpit. Space for 36 kg (80 lb) of baggage. Dual controls. Canopy optional
Construction: All-metal structure. Non-retractable landing gear

History: Thorp Engineering Company was founded by Mr John W. Thorp to market plans of his T-18 Tiger. The first T-18 to be completed was powered by a 134 kW (180 hp) Lycoming O-360 engine. Built by Mr W. Warwick, it flew for the first time on 12 May 1964. One T-18 built by Mr Ken Knowles of Palos Verdes, California, differs from the standard plans in having folding wings designed by Lon Sunderkind, with a shortened centre-section and lengthened outer wing panels to give a span of 7.67 m (25 ft 2 in), and is powered by a 101 kW (135 hp) Lycoming O-290 engine. This aircraft has a max level speed of 156 knots (290 km/h; 180 mph) and a range of 556 nm (1,030 km; 640 miles).
Several hundred sets of drawings have been sold and many T-18s are flying

For details: PO Box 516, Sun Valley, California 91352, USA.

(USA)

Two-seat sporting monoplane

Data: Turner T-40C
Power plant: One 112 kW (150 hp) Lycoming flat-four engine
Wing span: 8.53 m (28 ft 0 in)
Wing area, gross: 9.48 m² (102 sq ft)
Length overall: 6.12 m (20 ft 1 in)
Width, wings folded: 2.39 m (7 ft 10 in)
Height overall: 1.83 m (6 ft 0 in)
Weight empty: 376 kg (828 lb)
Max T-O weight: 748 kg (1,650 lb)
Max level speed at S/L: 165 knots (306 km/h; 190 mph)
Max cruising speed at S/L: 152 knots (282 km/h; 175 mph)
Max rate of climb at S/L: 457 m (1,500 ft)/min
Service ceiling, estimated: 6,400 m (21,000 ft)
Range with max payload, 20 min reserve: 521 nm (965 km; 600 miles)
Accommodation: Two seats side by side under rearward-sliding transparent canopy. Space for 22.5 kg (50 lb) of baggage aft of seats
Construction: All-wood structure, plywood covered, except for glassfibre tail-fin and engine cowling. Retractable landing gear

History: The T-40C is a derivative of the Turner T-40B, utilising that aircraft's fuselage and incorporating simplified model aeroplane-type construction. The wing has a highly modified and computer-developed version of the NASA GAW-2 supercritical section, known as TEDDE/2 supercritical. It incorporates a quick-release wing folding mechanism, with built-in electrical, flight control and seat-belt/shoulder harness interlock system. This is a fail-safe system, which prevents starting of the engine or actuation of the flight control system until the wings are unfolded and locked, as well as requiring the seatbelt/shoulder harness to be fastened.

Originally, Mr E.L. Turner designed and built a single-seat aircraft designated T-40. This first flew in April 1961, with a 63.5 kW (85 hp) engine, and was subsequently modified into the prototype of the two-seat T-40A, in which form it first flew in July 1966. In October of the same year the prototype was further modified into the T-40B, with a tricycle landing gear and other refinements. The first flight of the T-40B was made in March 1969. Flight tests showed the aircraft to be below expectation in high-altitude performance, and a 93 kW (125 hp) Lycoming O-320-E1C engine was installed. Later, in 1972, a bubble canopy was fitted. A Super T-40A aircraft, with increased wing span, a more powerful engine and other changes, flew for the first time in early 1972.

In 1975 Mr Turner's designs came under the control of an organisation named Turner Educational Development Enterprises (TEDDE). Approval for construction of the aircraft by amateur builders in Australia, the UK and West Germany was being sought in 1976

For details: PO Box 425, Stratford, Connecticut 06497, USA.

(USA)

Single-seat sporting monoplane

Power plant: One 93 kW (125 hp) Lycoming O-290-G (GPU) flat-four engine
Wing span: 6.07 m (19 ft 11 in)
Wing area, gross: 8.36 m² (90 sq ft)
Length overall: 5.79 m (19 ft 0 in)
Height overall: 1.55 m (5 ft 1 in)
Weight empty: 315 kg (695 lb)
Max T-O weight: 476 kg (1,050 lb)
Max level speed at S/L: 169 knots (314 km/h; 195 mph)
Max cruising speed at 2,440 m (8,000 ft): 161 knots (298 km/h; 185 mph)
Max rate of climb at S/L: 579 m (1,900 ft)/min
Service ceiling: 6,400 m (21,000 ft) •
Range, no reserve: 520 nm (965 km; 600 miles)

Accommodation: Single seat beneath transparent bubble canopy. Baggage space aft of seat
Construction: All-metal structure. Non-retractable landing gear

History: Design of the Van's RV-3 was started in 1968, by Mr Richard VanGrunsven. The prototype was built over a 2½-year period, at a cost of approximately $2,000, and won its designer the Best Aerodynamic Detailing award at the 1972 EAA Fly-in. In addition to trailing-edge flaps, the RV-3 has drooping ailerons to improve low-speed control.

After the RV-3's first flight, and subsequent EAA award, Van's Aircraft was formed to market plans to amateur constructors. By March 1976 a total of 340 sets of plans had been sold, with 100 aircraft reported to be under construction and eight RV-3s flying, including the prototype

For details: 22730 S W Francis, Beaverton, Oregon 97005, USA.

(USA)

VOLMER VJ-22 SPORTSMAN

Two-seat light amphibian

Data: Prototype with 63.5 kW (85 hp) engine
Power plant: One Continental C85 (63.5 kW; 85 hp) or Continental O-200-B (67 or 74.5 kW; 90 or 100 hp) flat-four engine
Wing span: 11.12 m (36 ft 6 in)
Wing area, gross: 16.3 m² (175 sq ft)
Length overall: 7.32 m (24 ft 0 in)
Height overall: 2.44 m (8 ft 0 in)
Weight empty: 454 kg (1,000 lb)
Max T-O weight: 680 kg (1,500 lb)
Max level speed at S/L: 83 knots (153 km/h; 95 mph)
Max cruising speed: 74 knots (137 km/h; 85 mph)
Max rate of climb at S/L: 183 m (600 ft)/min
Service ceiling: 3,960 m (13,000 ft)
Range with max fuel, no reserves: 260 nm (480 km; 300 miles)
Accommodation: Two seats side by side in enclosed cabin, with dual controls

Construction: Braced wings, with wooden spars and metal ribs, fabric covered. Wooden hull structure, covered with plywood and coated with glassfibre. Braced steel tube tail structure, fabric covered. Retractable landing gear

History: Mr Volmer Jensen designed and built the prototype Sportsman light amphibian, which flew for the first time on 22 December 1958 and has since logged over 1,600 flying hours. He is attempting to find a manufacturer who will produce and market the aircraft commercially.

Meanwhile, plans for the Sportsman are available to amateur constructors. Nearly 750 sets had been sold by the Spring of 1976, and approximately 100 Sportsman amphibians are flying. Some have tractor propellers, but this modification is disapproved of by Mr Jensen

For details: Box 5222 Glendale, California 91201, USA.

Two-seat sporting monoplane

Data: Standard version
Power plant: Any Continental or Lycoming flat-four engine between 48.5 and 93 kW (65 and 125 hp)
Wing span: 10.73 m (35 ft 2½ in)
Length overall: 6.82 m (22 ft 4½ in)
Height overall: 2.03 m (6 ft 8 in)
Weight empty: 314 kg (692 lb)
Max T-O weight: 608 kg (1,340 lb)
Max rate of climb at S/L: 89 knots (164 km/h; 102 mph)
Cruising speed: 82 knots (151 km/h; 94 mph)
Max rate of climb at S/L: 149 m (490 ft)/min
Service ceiling: 3,415 m (11,200 ft)
Range with standard fuel (45 litres, 12 US gallons): 191 nm (354 km; 220 miles)
Accommodation: Two seats in tandem in enclosed cockpit
Construction: Basically-wooden wing structure, with light alloy leading-edge and fabric covering. Fuselage and tail unit are of welded chrome molybdenum steel tube, with fabric covering. Non-retractable landing gear

History: Wag-Aero is making available to homebuilders plans and kits of parts to enable them to construct a modern version of the famous Piper Cub. Known as the CUBy, this aircraft follows the original design, but benefits by utilising up-to-date constructional techniques.
Also available is the CUBy Acro Trainer, which differs from the standard version by having shortened wings, modified lift struts, improved wing fittings and rib spacing, and a new leading-edge.
Design of the CUBy began in 1974, and construction of the prototype started in December of that year. First flight took place on 12 March 1975. By February 1976 plans for 154 CUBys had been ordered

For details: Box 181, 1216 North Road, Lyons, Wisconsin 53148, USA.

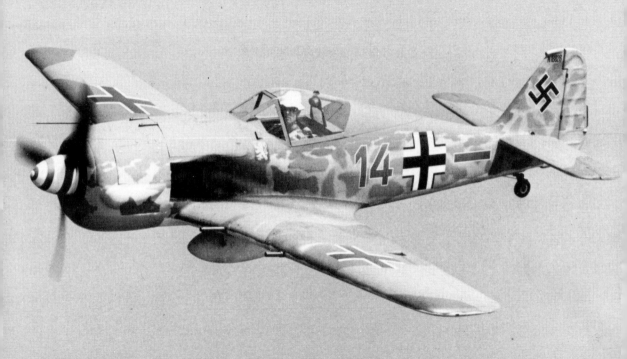

(USA)

Half-scale aircraft replica

Power plant: One 74.5 kW (100 hp) Continental O-200 flat-four engine
Wing span: 6.10 m (20 ft 0 in)
Wing area, gross: 6.50 m² (70 sq ft)
Length overall: 5.05 m (16 ft 7 in)
Height overall: 2.13 m (7 ft 0 in)
Weight empty: 286 kg (630 lb)
Max T-O weight: 408 kg (900 lb)
Max level speed at 1,065 m (3,500 ft): 160 knots (298 km/h; 185 mph)
Max cruising speed, above height: 126 knots (233 km/h; 145 mph).
Max rate of climb at S/L: 305 m (1,000 ft)/min
Service ceiling: 3,810 m (12,500 ft)
Range with max fuel: 347 nm (643 km; 400 miles)
Accommodation: Single-seat beneath rearward-sliding cockpit canopy
Construction: Wooden primary wing structure, with a laminated hollow plywood-covered front spar and solid laminated rear spar.

WAR AIRCRAFT REPLICAS FOCKE-WULF 190

Plywood and polyurethane foam wing ribs. Aerofoil contours built up with carved polyurethane foam. High-strength laminating fabric and epoxy resin used for covering. Fuselage of similar general construction to wings, with a standard wooden box, plywood covered, and a metal-faced plywood firewall. Contours built up with carved polyurethane foam, fabric/epoxy covered. Tail unit construction similar to that of wings. Retractable landing gear

History: War Aircraft Replicas is a company formed to market plans and kits from which amateur constructors can build ½-scale replicas of Second World War aircraft. The term ½-scale is not strictly accurate, but refers to the general overall dimensions of the aircraft. The Focke-Wulf 190 was chosen as the first prototype to be completed, its design starting in July 1973 and construction in February 1974. The first flight of this aircraft was made on 21 August 1974, and 60 sets of plans had been sold by 1976. By this time the prototype had accumulated 200 flying hours. Other types, such as the Vought F4U Corsair fighter, are under construction, using the same basic fuselage box and wing structure as the Focke-Wulf 190

For details: 348 South Eighth Street, Santa Paula, California 93060, USA.

Focke-Wulf 190 with 74.5 kW (100 hp) Continental O-200 engine

Single-seat sporting biplane

Data: Prototype with 86 kW (115 hp) Lycoming engine
Power plant: One 86 kW (115 hp) Lycoming O-235-C1 flat-four engine. Structure will accept alternative power plants, from 1,600 cc Volkswagen up to 112 kW (150 hp) flat-four engines
Wing span: upper   6.10 m (20 ft 0 in)
                 lower   4.88 m (16 ft 0 in)
Wing area, gross: 10.68 m² (115 sq ft)
Length overall: 5.18 m (17 ft 0 in)
Weight empty: 242 kg (534 lb)
Max T-O weight: 403 kg (888 lb)
Max level speed at 610 m (2,000 ft): 126 knots (233 km/h; 145 mph)
Max cruising speed at 610 m (2,000 ft): 116 knots (214 km/h; 133 mph)
Max rate of climb at S/L: 732 m (2,400 ft)/min
Accommodation: Single seat in open cockpit
Construction: Wooden wing structure, fabric covered, with internal steel tube bracing. Welded steel tube fuselage structure, fabric covered. Aluminium engine cowling. Wood or glassfibre fuselage turtleback. Braced metal tail unit, fabric covered. Non-retractable landing gear

History: Marshall White, designer of this aircraft, named it Der Jäger D.IX because it is reminiscent of German aircraft of First World War vintage. The wings are patterned on those of an Albatros D.Va, with the landing gear fairings of the later Focke-Wulf Stösser and tail unit of the Fokker D.VII.
Design and construction of the prototype started simultaneously at the beginning of 1969, as Mr White's fifth homebuilt, and first flight of the prototype was made on 7 September 1969.
Plans and kits of materials, as well as some of the more difficult-to-construct parts in finished form, are available to amateur constructors. At least 75 Der Jäger D.IXs are under construction, with the first of them nearing completion in 1976.
The prototype has been re-engined with a 112 kW (150 hp) Lycoming power plant, but performance data with this engine were not available in mid-1976

For details: Meadowlark Airport, 5141 Warner Avenue, Huntington Beach, California 92649, USA.

Single-seat ultra-light monoplane

Power plant: One 41 kW (55 hp) 1,600 cc Volkswagen engine
Wing span: 7.32 m (24 ft 0 in)
Wing area, gross: 8.83 m ^{2} (95.0 sq ft)
Length overall: 5.49 m (18 ft 0 in)
Height overall: 1.60 m (5 ft 3 in)
Weight empty: 258.5 kg (570 lb)
Max T-O weight: 385.5 kg (850 lb)
Max level speed, estimated: 96 knots (177 km/h; 110 mph)
Max cruising speed, estimated: 83 knots (153 km/h; 95 mph)
Max rate of climb at S/L, estimated: 152 m (500 ft)/min
Service ceiling, estimated: 4,265 m (14,000 ft)
Range with max fuel, estimated: 173 nm (320 km; 200 miles)
Accommodation: Single seat under flush moulded canopy. Bag-gage space aft of seat

Construction: Aluminium alloy and glassfibre stressed-skin wing structure. Pod-type central fuselage nacelle, consisting of moulded glassfibre shell carried on an aluminium alloy box beam. Twin aluminium alloy beams carry tail. Aluminium alloy tail structure, with glassfibre fairings. Propeller shrouded by annular duct. Non-retractable landing gear

History: Mr Whittaker has completed the prototype of his MW2 design for a single-seat aircraft. Named the Excalibur, design work began in 1972 and construction started in September 1974; first flight of this aircraft was due to take place in the Summer of 1976.
The prototype has been stressed to BCAR (K) requirements, and it is intended to obtain PFA certification initially; CAA certification will be sought before any series production is undertaken

(USA/UK)

Two-seat cabin monoplane

Data: Standard W-8 Tailwind built to Wittman plans, with 74.5 kW (100 hp) Continental engine
Power plant: Normally one 67 kW (90 hp) Continental C90-12F flat-four engine. Alternative engines are 63.4 kW (85 hp) Continental C85, 74.5 kW (100 hp) Continental O-200, 86 kW (115 hp) Lycoming O-235 or 104.5 kW (140 hp) Lycoming O-290
Wing span: 6.86 m (22 ft 6 in)
Wing area, gross: 8.36 m² (90 sq ft)
Length overall: 5.87 m (19 ft 3 in)
Height overall: 1.73 m (5 ft 8 in)
Weight empty: 318 kg (700 lb)
Max T-O weight: 590 kg (1,300 lb)
Max level speed at S/L: 143 knots (265 km/h; 165 mph)
Max cruising speed: 139 knots (257 km/h; 160 mph)
Max rate of climb at S/L: 275 m (900 ft)/min
Service ceiling: 4,876 m (16,000 ft)
Range with max payload at 3,050 m (10,000 ft), no reserve, at 139 knots (257 km/h; 160 mph): 521 nm (965 km; 600 miles)
Accommodation: Two seats side by side in enclosed cabin, with door on each side. Space for 27 kg (60 lb) baggage
Construction: Braced wings of wooden construction, with plywood and fabric covering. Ailerons and flaps of steel and stainless steel construction. Steel tube fuselage structure, fabric covered. Cantilever tail unit of steel and stainless steel construction. Non-retractable landing gear.

History: Steve Wittman, famous as a racing pilot since 1926, has designed and built a large number of aircraft, the most popular current design being the Tailwind. The prototype was built in 1952-53 and proved so successful that sets of plans and prefabricated components were made available to amateur constructors. By the Spring of 1972 there were more than 150 Model W-8 Tailwinds flying, including a number built abroad, and more than 100 were known to be under construction.

In 1966, a more powerful 108 kW (145 hp) Continental O-300 flat-six engine was installed in a Tailwind, redesigned to take the added weight and power. This version is designated W-9 and has a max speed of 172 knots (319 km/h; 198 mph).

AJEP Developments is marketing in the UK plans and construction kits for a modified version of the Wittman Tailwind, two examples of which were completed by early 1976. Design changes include a revised tail unit with swept vertical and horizontal surfaces, modified engine cowling, and revised wing section. Several internal modifications have also been made

For details: Box 276, Oshkosh, Wisconsin 54901, USA.
AJEP Developments: The Lodge, Marden Hill Farm, nr Hertford, Hertfordshire SG14 2NE, England

AJEP Tailwind

(Canada)

Two-seat all-metal light monoplane

Power plant: One 74.5 kW (100 hp) Rolls-Royce Continental O-200-A flat-four engine in prototype. Design suitable for engines from 63.4 kW (85 hp) to 119 kW (160 hp)
Wing span: 7.00 m (22 ft 11¾ in)
Wing area, gross: 9.80 m² (105.9 sq ft)
Length overall: 6.30 m (20 ft 8 in)
Height overall: 1.85 m (6 ft 0¾ in)
Weight empty, equipped: 400 kg (881 lb)
Normal T-O and landing weight: 650 kg (1,433 lb)
Max T-O weight: 680 kg (1,499 lb)
Max level speed at S/L: 126 knots (233 km/h; 145 mph)
Cruising speed (75% power) at 2,750 m (9,000 ft): 116 knots (215 km/h; 134 mph)
Max rate of climb at S/L: 240 m (787 ft)/min
Service ceiling: 4,600 m (15,100 ft)
Range with max fuel, no reserves (75% power): 432 nm (800 km; 497 miles)
Accommodation: Two seats side by side under sideways-opening Plexiglas canopy. Dual controls, with single column located centrally between seats. Space for 35 kg (77 lb) of baggage aft of seats. Cabin heated and ventilated
Construction: Aluminium alloy structure with aluminium alloy skin. Non-retractable landing gear

History: M Heintz, a professional aeronautical engineer, participated in the design of several of the aircraft produced by Avions Pierre Robin. While in France, he also designed and built the prototype of a two-seat light aircraft named the Zénith, intended for amateur construction.

Work on the Zénith began in October 1968; the prototype first flew on 22 March 1970 and was granted French CNRA (homebuilt experimental aircraft) certification. In October 1970 the original wing was replaced by one with a section offering improved low-speed characteristics.

In June 1971, the prototype won a handicap race at Iverdon, Switzerland, at an average speed of 124 knots (230 km/h; 143 mph) from a standing start. In 1974 the Zénith was granted the US National Association of Sport Aircraft Designers (NASAD) 'seal of quality' No 108.

Sets of plans and a constructional manual for the Zénith, with engines between 63.4 and 119 kW (85 and 160 hp), are available to amateur builders from the sources listed below. By early 1976 more than 300 sets of plans had been sold in all parts of the world, and several aircraft were flying in Europe and North America.

The single-seat Mono Zénith and three-seat Tri-Zénith are variations of the same basic design

For details: 236 Richmond Street, Richmond Hill L4C 3Y8, Ontario, Canada.
France: French manual and metric measurements from D. Triques, 23 Av Edouard Belin, Foutaine d'Ouche F.21, Dijon, France.
Germany: German manual and metric measurements from K. Arens, Rollstrasse 26, D-3392 Clausthal-Zellerfeld 1, Germany.
USA and Canada: As above, Zenair also offering materials, parts and complete kits.

Zenith with 74.5 kW (100 hp) Continental engine

INDEX

INDEX

INDEX

1933-73